THREE MONTHS IN PENNSYLVANIA

DIARY OF A FREEDOM FIGHTER

Three Months in Pennsylvania

Diary of a Freedom Fighter

Suzanne Cruz

ISBN: 978-1-944878-29-0

This book is dedicated to Morton, the donors, and trainers for which the trip, education, and adventure would not have been possible. Thank you for the opportunity to serve this great country in the manner of which you have provided.

And to my grandson Joshua. As Reagan said, "Liberty and freedom is every generation's fight."

CONTENTS

TIME FOR CHANGE

"Life begins when we get out of our comfort zone."

—Suzanne Cruz

There is a thing that happens to people as they age. A lethargy over-comes them, and it can manifest itself on their bodies or in their minds as they prepare for the end. Now, with fewer years in front of them than behind, they begin to slow down. Many of my friends who had reached the half-century mark could be heard saying with increasing fre-quency, "I'm old, I am tired." They had stopped growing. These common and familiar phrases, I believe, were used as a way to be excused from a life they had grown tired of. They had fought their battles. The new battles and battles of the future? Why, those were for the young to fight—not them. They had fought theirs. Personally, I knew I was certainly tired of the fighting, but I also knew I was not dead either. Then I was offered a job that changed me and the Commonwealth of Pennsylvania too. This is our story.

BRACE YOURSELF FOR WAR

"We fight, get beat, rise, and fight again."

—Nathanael Greene, Washington's First Lieutenant

The year is 2016, the month is August. For a year now the fighting has been intense, and is now getting ugly. An election is in front of America for the President of the United States. We are divided, and the fighting has been as vicious as it was in 1863. It is a civil war, only civilly decided with ballots and not bullets. This is one of the ugliest elections I have witnessed in my lifetime. National arguments and wounds long ago settled have been ripped open. We are a nation weary and weak from the fighting. As the political pundits work to divide us in an effort to get "their" candidate to win, they bear direct responsibility for stirring up animosities and the blood bath that follows. We were losing the greatest experiment in the history of the world. At this time, I decided to physically enter the battlefield. Very bad people are calling this nation a bad country—there is something sick about that. The scream of "racism" is so loud it's deafening. To call America racist; it is the least racist project in human history. There is nothing like this. A soullessness has come over this country—one that emanates from boredom, created by the death of God and religion, and the combination of affluence, freedom and secularism has been devastating on its people. November eighth, it will be settled. There will be a side that wins and a side that has lost. God help us all.

I was offered a job as a field rep at precisely this time—the time of fierce fighting. A field rep is kind of like a Jehovah's Witness; we visit universities and sit and wait for students to come by and tell them how awesome America is. I am not kidding you. People pay me for this. As students walk by, a conversation is begun about this topic. Inevitably and with stunning frequency, the student reveals that they had just come from some class where their professor had just told them what a piece of shit America is. Or how they were targeted sometimes for their conservative or Christian beliefs. How they were mocked, ridiculed, and even threatened by other students or downgraded in their classes. That is where I inform the student of the difference between an indoctrination and an education. That tolerance and diversity also applies to them. That if they took a biology class, they should get a biology class, and not some rant about why their professor hates Ronald Reagan.

We are evangelists set out to reform campuses coast to coast, one person at a time. Our job is to rescue the marginalized and dismissed youth, a sort of Saving Private Ryan if you will, to form clubs so that they can build strength and create a sense of unity and belonging within the walls of academia, so they are not lost and absorbed by those that would want to indoctrinate rather than educate.

There are conservative professors as well who have been just as mistreated and are grateful for strength that comes from having students united in defense of their values. Viktor Frankl had it right: besides food, the biggest human urge is meaning. There are people who live without sex and have a happy life, but there is not one who lives without meaning. We go onto campuses and help students and teachers realize that they and their ideas have meaning.

MY TRAINING BEGINS

"If men were angels, no government would be necessary. If angels were to govern men, neither external nor internal controls on government would be necessary. In framing a government which is to be administered by men over men, the great difficulty lies in this: you must first enable the government to control the governed; and in the next place oblige it to control itself."

—Alexander Hamilton

Arlington, Virginia. Up to this point you must understand I was a hotel and taxi person. I had no idea what Uber was, nor Airbnb. And of course, when the plane landed, I called a taxi. It was very dark, and only the city lights were visible to me. I jumped into the dark cab, he took my bags, and we were off. I was still excited, even though I could not see a thing. I talked and talked like a small child being taken to the circus for the first time. He tolerated me, grunting and nodding, absorbed in the monotony of his job. Seeing that he was not amused at my antics or chatter, I spent the rest of the trip in silence, simply watching and marveling at all the new sites, as dark as it was. By the time we got to the hotel I had been in motion, traveling across the United States for the better part of 12 hours. I fell into bed and pulled the covers over my head. The beauty of Virginia would not reveal herself to me until the morning.

That very first morning, a small slit of light beamed into my eyes. I jumped up and flung open the draperies. Virginia was a different world, green and lush. Grass grew everywhere, which is an incredibly stark difference from the State of California that seems to be forever on fire. I pulled on my jogging clothes, placed a small day satchel over my shoulder, and sprinted out the door of the hotel to greet this new world. But then I came back in because I did not know where in the heck I was. After some conferencing with the hotel clerk and getting a couple of maps, I had a direction. I would take the subway, again a first in my life, and head to Washington D.C only a few miles away.

"Really? You're kidding me. It's that close?" This guy could have been related to the taxi cab driver, I thought. He crinkled his eyebrows and seemed suspect at my innocent and juvenile fascination with this old town. He was probably wondering where my minder was.

I was off and running, although the humidity had to have been 73%. I didn't care. I was in love with this whole area—the green, the architecture, the colossal churches, the constant buzzing of the cicadas, even the grouchy hotel clerk and indifferent taxi driver. I felt like Marlo Thomas, and if I had a hat, I would have flung it in the air. I had only this day to see everything; the rest of the week I would be in a classroom morning till night. I had to make the most of every second, so I jogged. I jogged all day and all over the National Mall until my feet ached. It was not much of a tour, but I saw a lot as it went whizzing past. Up to the Lincoln Memorial, past the Jefferson Memorial, West Potomac Park, Constitution Gardens, and the Washington Monument, as well as most of the war memorials. My legs gave out. Around the time I reached the White House, I collapsed on the lawn and fell asleep, and only woke to the sound of an Indian family arguing over who lost the kid.

TRAINING

"A free people ought not only to be armed, but disciplined; to which end a uniform and well-digested plan is requisite; and their safety and interest require that they should promote such manufactories as tend to render them independent of others for essential, particularly military, supplies."

—George Washington

That Monday I started school. I stayed in Arlington for a week of "training," and honestly, I had no idea what I was getting trained for. I felt awesome at my age—I was fit! I exercised hard five days a week, ate a dark green salad with protein every day, and got plenty of sleep. I felt thirty years old. I thought I looked thirty years old. Then, once I got in the classroom, I realized they had made a mistake. I looked around at the other fifty students. They had to be between nineteen and thirty years old. I thought to myself, *Well, Suzanne, you might feel thirty, but nope, clearly you are fifty.*

The days were long; training us would take a week. The object was to give us enough information to operate on our own with little to no supervision for three months, so every possible scenario would have to be addressed.

First, a history on the radicals you will encounter. Saul Alinsky, author of *Rules for Radicals*, is a guide for the community organizer to unite low-income communities. Alinsky makes a strong case for the abandonment of morals and ethics as nothing but impediments to political success. For Alinsky, ethics prevent the world from being what "it should be." The Alinsky end game is likely a global utopia in which the "people" have "power." Unfortunately, this utopianism has been the foundation of several über-violent movements of the last century, which have resulted in over 100 million deaths.

Next we study the Constitution: why it is not a living document, nor was it ever intended to be. We learn how to find and interact with students, how to listen to people, and how to help students find legal help if they have been mistreated and ostracized on campus. We study how to put on activism events, how to hire speakers, and read books that support the ideologies of the Founding Fathers. We spend a lot of time on limited government, fiscal responsibility, and what it takes to run the best and most moral economy that looks out for the best interests of the most number of people. Since there is no perfect system, nor will there ever be till the second coming of Christ, we ask again and again: what is the system that is the most moral and fair to the most amount of people?

It is our job to find these students that align with this thought and unite them with each other. That is it. It's kind of like Match.com.

UBER

It's not tyranny we desire; it's a just, limited, federal government.

—Alexander Hamilton, first Treasury Secretary

We broke for dinner early and I had bonded with a couple of younger gals. That would be the other four of us, as the rest of the class was all male. It's kind of neat being the old gal. You don't have to conform anymore. If you dress weird, you're forgiven 'cause your older and girls call you sweet. If you say something caustic, you're forgiven 'cause your old and grouchy. That night was my very first night in an Uber, and as we left the restaurant I was stunned to see the line of unused taxis with drivers leaning up against their cars, just as surely as the one I had met the night at the airport. They were all smoking and talking, but not in service. Why? Because a phenomenon was happening. People using their own personal vehicles as taxis had become Uber drivers. A steady stream of moms and dads in sedans and mini vans picked people up from some of the fanciest restaurants. Even people that could afford to pay more for a taxi were not using them. Why? The reason had just as much to do with social reasons as it did cost savings.

As the girls and I crammed in the Uber driver's car, we were greeted by an astonishing difference—the driver was happy! We all chatted up a storm and exchanged information about everything under the sun. The driver was a black woman and we were all white women, and by the time we got to the hotel we were laughing so hard we were wiping tears from our faces. In the end, we were exchanging names like old friends. This phenomenon did not happen once, but every single time we used an Uber. We met Hindu men, Vietnamese college students, and an Indian man who expressed again and again how great America was.

A news topic I had not paid attention to up to that point now came screaming to the forefront of my mind. There were a few states who had been pressured by cab companies to regulate Uber out of existence! What a crime this would be; how un-American this would be. In a divided nation, this was the salve that we needed: more opportunities to work together in mutual benefit. In exchange for a ride in your car, I give you money. We are both happy and both retain our dignity in our ability to earn extra cash and the opportunity to be kind to a total stranger. The friendlier the driver was, the higher their ratings went. It was the free and moral market at work. And now those that are for big government wanted to regulate it out of existence. I added this to my list of things I wanted to fight.

HOME TO PACK

"I must study politics and war that my sons may have liberty to study mathematics and philosophy"

—John Adams

By the end of the week, most of us had the states we requested. I had requested Virginia since I had always wanted to live on the east coast and see the magnificent changing of the seasons I had heard so much about. I had dreamed of living in Virginia for a very long time, but was asked to go to Pennsylvania instead, since Virginia was taken. Unbeknownst to me, it would be one of the happiest disappointments of my life. I called an Uber driver who took me to the airport, and then headed west, home to California.

It was not perhaps the best time to leave, but when is? I was a grandma-to-be; my daughter and her husband would be expecting their first child in four months. My husband was very accomplished and capable, but of course, he was not happy about me leaving for three months. He, being much older than me, had already had his adventures. He had designed and built his own ocean-going sailboat, traveled the South Pacific visiting Fiji and French Polynesian islands, and finally settled in New Zealand where he lived for several years. He was an accomplished musician, land surveyor, and champion swimmer. He knew I needed this, and so reluctantly helped me pack. Dick helped me with everything, actually—maps, shopping, and researching the area for the best place to live. I had been encouraged to find a long-term Airbnb. I had never used one before, so I was unsure. We decided that Mechanicsburg would be a good central location and found one right there on main street.

Part of the adventure would be driving from California to Pennsylvania. It was both part of the fun and part of the necessity. I would need my car when I got there. I got rid of my old car, bought a new one, packed it with enough basic clothes for three months, and enough food to travel across the United States. I would take the Lincoln Highway across eight states: Nevada, Utah, Wyoming, Nebraska, Iowa, Illinois, Indiana, Ohio, and finally, into Pennsylvania. And I did bring my little friend, Smith and Wesson, so I was not completely alone.

By the end of a week of driving, I was well done in, used to working out six days a week and being on a strict diet of little more than kale and protein. I was getting none of that. The closer I got to Pennsylvania, the more often I was offered bagels and cream cheese. Finding a gym was near impossible, so when I went to hotels that did not have a gym, I ran around the parking lot about two-hundred and six times. When I stayed at an Airbnb where there would be no exercise room, I dropped and did about fifty pushups, and then would park at the farthest ends of parking lots to jog to my destination. Sometimes, when I was in a long line at a store, I would lean up against a candy shelving unit and sneak in a few arm dips. I got used to the odd looks from other customers.

YOU'VE ARRIVED

"I am determined to be cheerful and happy in whatever situation I may find myself. For I have learned that the greater part of our misery or unhappiness is determined not by our circumstance but by our disposition."

—Martha Washington

Welcome to Pennsylvania, the sign read. I had crossed the border! Quakers arrived in this area in 1681 as a religious refuge. The territory now known as Pennsylvania was given to William Penn by King Charles II of England as a royal Charter. Later this state would have enormous roles in the American Revolution, The Civil War, and its largest city, Philadelphia, would house the first Nations Capitol, Independence Hall, for much of the nineteenth century. Pennsylvania was the second state admitted into the union. Rich with history, it was the perfect place for a history buff like me. As I traveled to the Airbnb I had rented for three months, I marveled at the green grass. There was not a brown weed anywhere. There was so much grass that even the highway islands were mowed!

The place I had rented was humorously named "The Tarzan Hut." I had an idea what it would look like when I was in California, but you know how it goes from the image you have in your head to actually seeing and experiencing something. It was not as charming as I had imagined—a big brown box that sat atop a garage. It was in old town Mechanicsburg. There were stories of the Civil War spilling into even these streets, and not just nearby Gettysburg. The apartment across the small street was at least one hundred years old; with broken windows and faded white paint, it was a little creepy.

I pulled in about eight in the evening and met my new landlord, Benjamin. He was a roundish man of about seventy-five, with thinning hair and a thick Jewish accent. We shook each other's hands and he ushered me inside his home, where I met his wife—a cute, sexy, Filipino woman about twenty years his junior. I don't know why it stunned me to see this mismatch, but I was seldom one without something to say, and I found myself at a loss for words. I said, "Hell, Hell, Hell, Hello, so nice to meet you." We enjoyed tea and cookies in the dining room where we played a game of "who are you and why are you here?" I think I passed. They liked me, because a few minutes later we were all working to haul my stuff up those crazy narrow spiral stairs up to my Tarzan Hut for the next three months. As Benjamin swung open the door, a smile of pride came over his face as he presented the room to me. It was a square room with old and faded tan carpet, and a small kitchenette tucked in the corner with a hotplate and microwave. The bed had a Hawaiian flower quilt on it, with red geometric designed pillowcases and yellow sheets. The bathroom was small with the same tan, worn carpet. A florescent, psychedelic striped pattern towel ensemble adorned the towel rack. It was the most Gawde awful example of poor decorating taste I had ever seen in my whole life. Most of the furniture was creaky old 1940s mismatch, thrown in with a pressboard TV stand. Benjamin left and I sat on the bed. After nearly a week of travel, I was glad to be sitting still. I sighed and then let myself go all the way into the bed. It creaked and I groaned. Home for the next three months, this was the most beautiful place on earth right now, and I fell asleep.

BAPTISM BY FIRE,
MY FIRST DAY OF WORK

"They tell us, sir, that we are weak; unable to cope with so formidable an adversary. But when shall we be stronger? Will it be the next week, or the next year? Will it be when we are totally disarmed, and when a British guard shall be stationed in every house? Shall we gather strength by irresolution and inaction? Shall we acquire the means of effectual resistance by lying supinely on our backs and hugging the delusive phantom of hope, until our enemies shall have bound us hand and foot? Sir, we are not weak if we make a proper use of those means which the God of nature hath placed in our power."

—Patrick Henry

I met my very first Communist today. While working at a student involvement fair with the Young Americans for Liberty, a Libertarian group, at the University of Pennsylvania in Pittsburgh, it was as if he had been suckled on the Communist Manifesto.

He came up to our table and began a conversation with me. For every reason I told him Capitalism was moral, he would fire back with complete confidence why it was not. He was tall, about six-foot two, blonde, handsome, and fairly articulate about his reasoning. We are taught not to argue, since our mission is to gather up those who are likeminded. If you stand there and argue with these kinds of people, you are going to lose those potential club members as they walk past, defeating your purpose. So, I had to let him go. Besides that, about the time it started getting heated, his little ankle-biting girlfriend came up and began to snarl and snap at me. "Yeah, yeah, he is right."

By the end of the day, we got about two hundred sign ups—not bad for a university with a population of twenty thousand. As I left that day, with my backpack full of books slung across my back, my voice hoarse and body tired, my mind was wracked with anguish towards that one Communist. What part of history did he think he was paying for but was not getting? My mind went back to the year 1847, the year Karl Marx dumped his work, the Communist Manifesto, onto the world. America would be on her eleventh president, Polk, and embroiled in the Mexican-American War. Lincoln would have been an Illinois state representative and against this war, and another revolution was in full swing—the industrial one.

The irony of this whole Communist thing is that while the university professors whip up feelings of envy towards the "haves," students ignore the fact that the very tenured professors with fat pensions and fancy cars and nice houses, are the haves.

What was fascinating about the Industrial Revolution that spawned envy and Karl, was that it made people's lives better, but as all revolutions go there are things, people, and ideas that die, and those that are set free. If you did not adapt to capitalism, you would be run over. Karl was one of those ones who got run over. He struggled financially, refused to get a job, and let his family starve or die one by one. It was someone else's fault, and so, in anger and frustration, he wrote this work outlining how others could force others to work and give up their stuff so others could benefit from the work of others. If anyone refused to participate in the grand sharing, redistribution, and government benevolence scheme they would be forced or killed. Stalin liked this idea, and today so do North Korea and China.

I continued to scratch my head all the way to my car until I had rubbed raw a bald spot.

ANOTHER MAN'S PERSPECTIVE

"Knowledge will forever govern ignorance; and a people who mean to be their own governors must arm themselves with the power which knowledge gives."

—James Madison 1791

In 1847 Karl Marx was both frustrated and furious with the crushing arm of capitalism that swept through Europe, forcing people to conform or be crushed. But another person across the pond had a different reaction to the Industrial Revolution—a Scottish immigrant and a child laborer. Little Andy Carnegie saw the possibilities. It is not possible to be in Pittsburgh, Pennsylvania without either hearing or seeing the name Andrew Carnegie. Who was he, and why is he so important to this area? Was he the reason I had run into the junior Communist? Was a he a vile Robber Barron? I went to the Carnegie Library in Pittsburgh and read.

Andrew Carnegie, a Scottish immigrant, arrived in Pittsburgh Pennsylvania as a small child with his parents and brother. His father, a weaver, had been pushed out of a job by the new mechanized power loom. Other craftsmen and women had moved to the cities of England for work, since their slow method of clothmaking had become obsolete. But Andrew's father, like Karl Marx, refused to adapt, and so the family moved to America where they heard there were greater opportunities. It seems to me at this point during the great revolution, there were two trains of thought—either embrace and change as an individual, or resent and control others. History shows that those that embraced change and educated themselves adapted. Carnegie arrived penniless and went to work as a child laborer, but kept adapting and educating himself. He moved from telegraph courier, to railroad manager, to investor. He was an abolitionist and supported Lincoln's cause to end slavery. Carnegie served in the War Department, reorganizing telegraph service for the Union Army. He eventually educated himself on investing, and invested in the sleeper car. That was his first realization that money can work for you, rather than you physically working for it. He then invested in iron, and shortly after that the creation of steel from pig iron revolutionized construction. This allowed substantial bridges, buildings and railroads to be built. As his fortune grew, he reinvested it back into the world, giving libraries, colleges, museums and endowments back into communities.

His motto was, "Any wealthy man that dies with his money is a disgrace."

Upon reflection, I see that he lived what the founders wanted—private ownership, market freedom and reliable money. In doing so, he created work for people and enhanced the lives of many. None of this was done under bureaucratic order. I had a new understanding for the free market, a new respect for Carnegie, and a new consternation for Communism.

DIVISIONS AT
DELAWARE VALLEY

"There is nothing which I dread so much as a division of the republic into two great parties, each arranged under its leader, and concerting measures in opposition to each other. This in my humble apprehension is to be dreaded as the greatest political evil under our Constitution."

—John Adams

Delaware Valley University, an agricultural school, was not as large a club rush as I had hoped it would be, but the Young Americans for Liberty rep. Tom Carey asked me to go and help, so I did. I was glad I did, because I did meet one of my requirements—I created a Second Amendment group with a girl as a leader! Awesome! She is great, perky, and vibrant, but I forget her name just now. Anyway, at the days end I rented an Airbnb in Doylestown. It was late and getting dark, so I went right to my home for the night and met with Freida. Something fascinating about liberals and conservatives—we can tell each other apart. The old ones look old and haggard and resentful. The young ones at the colleges are not, however. They seem to be liberal because either some old matriarch told them they should be, or that they were told it was the "nicer way to be." In any case, I met an old one: Freida. She opened the door with the big required-and-expected smile of a host. I cracked a joke about my husband running our Airbnb and spending the same amount of money on food and extras as he was charging them. She did not laugh. She smirked and said, "Well, that is not happening here!" I knew I was toast. She brought me outside to her friend who was waiting for us on the porch to do the usual interrogation of a new guest. She was blond and looked like she had either been sick or had used meth at some point in her life. They asked me where I was from and I said I had escaped California, a third generation. "Escaped," they scoffed. "Are you mad? California is beautiful!" It was going downhill fast. After their little barbs at me regarding my failure to know California, they moved on to what I was doing in Pennsylvania. I realized that they knew just like I did, that from the mere look of me, I was conservative, and so the friend began her assault. Frieda allowing her to. After all, it was not that she was about to grill me, but her friend of whom she had no responsibility. In a matter of a few words on my part, "Wealth creation and limited government."

The friend says, "Oh, you're a right winger." Down came the hammer of judgment, and labels that I hated so much.

"Look," I said, "our mission is not to divide, it is to encourage the original ideas of the Founding Fathers of limited government. We need to stop labeling each other and look at the facts, to critically think."

Washington even told us to be wary of divisions in his farewell speech. It went something like this.

> "It serves always to distract the Public Councils, and enfeeble the Public Administration. It agitates the Community with ill-founded jealousies and false alarms; kindles the animosity of one part against another, foments occasionally riot and insurrection. It opens the door to foreign influence and corruption, which find a facilitated access to the government itself through the channels of party passions. Thus the policy and the will of one country are subjected to the policy and will of another.............. A fire not to be quenched, it demands a uniform vigilance to prevent its bursting into a flame, lest, instead of warming, it should consume."

There was silence after I recited this—a dead and uncomfortable silence. Frieda's friend reminded me of the taxi cab driver, a sour look on her face and bored with life, and waiting until I got out of the cab. It was over. I wanted to go to bed. They had spent years grooming their dark side, and Frieda, seeing it was going to get ugly fast, said, "Let's just all go to bed." In a heartbeat, I grabbed my bag and went inside. I hope I get credit in heaven for biting my tongue, because right then it was bleeding.

It was better in the morning. I had packed at 5:30 a.m., brushed my teeth, threw my hair up, put on my sneakers, and sprinted out the front door. I headed straight towards downtown Doylestown, the most charming and cutest old German town you ever want to see.

THE IRONY OF IT ALL

"Suppose you were an idiot, and suppose you were a member of Congress; but I repeat myself."

—Mark Twain 1865

I noticed in the local paper that Pennsylvania is debating a bathroom bill, HB1510 and SB974. Other states such as Maine and Washington have introduced new bathroom laws triggering a backfire effect. Both of those states have opened schools, public buildings, and businesses up to lawsuits by lawyers looking to line their pockets by doing so. The irony is that Pennsylvania was founded on the belief that government should get the hell out of people's business, both in the church and certainly in private matters such as where one should relieve themselves. The older I get, the more I realize how brilliant the founders were. They knew the human condition was to grab more power; that power likes to expand and this intrusion into people's private lives is testimony to their hindsight. So close to Independence Hall, it is ironic that Pennsylvania would not think independently and be guilty of group think.

"Time is what we want most, but what we use worst, right is right even if everyone is against it and wrong is wrong even if everyone is for it. In all debates let truth be thy aim, not victory or an unjust interest"

William Penn -1700

ORGANIZE, STRATEGIZE AND HYPOTHISIZE

"Four Score and Seven Years ago, our fathers brought forth on this continent a new nation, conceived in liberty, and dedicated to the proposition that all men are created equal. Now we are engaged in a great civil war, testing whether that nation or any nation so conceived and so dedicated, can long endure. We are met on a great battlefield of that war. We have come to dedicate a portion of that field, as a final resting place for those who gave their lives. It is altogether fitting and proper that we should do this.

But in a larger sense, we cannot dedicate, we cannot consecrate, we cannot hallow this ground. The brave men, living and dead who struggled here, have consecrated it, far about our poor power to add or detract. The world will little note, nor long remember what we say here, but it can never forget what they did here. It is for us the living rather, to be dedicated here to the unfinished work which they who fought here have thus far so nobly advanced. It is rather for us to be here dedicated to the great task remaining before us- that from these honored dead we take increased devotion to the cause for which they gave the last full measure of devotion- that we here highly resolve that these dead shall not have died in vain- that this nation under God, shall have a new birth of freedom-and that government of the people, by the people for the people, Shall not parish from the earth."

—Abraham Lincoln Nov. 19th 1863

Each day I must research and organize the next day. It is difficult to plan a whole week, because you never know which of the twenty clubs might want you to help them recruit members or put on an activism awareness event. If a student does ask for your help, it is most always a last-minute thing, and you drop everything else and go running. This was the case at the University of Gettysburg. As also is the case, I research what type of campus I am headed into. Will there be opposition to freedom and the First Amendment there? Will administration be present, treating adults like children and monitor each word spoken and each candy passed out? To find out, I check the FIRE rating, The Foundation for Individual Rights in Education. An overwhelming majority of colleges and universities across the country deny students the rights they are granted under the First Amendment or institutional promises. Every year FIRE reads through the rules government student speech at more than 400 of our nation's biggest and most prestigious universities to document the institutions that ignore students' rights or don't tell the truth about how they have taken them away. The FIRE spotlight database will tell me if Gettysburg is one of them. I hold my breath and look. It's RED. I cannot believe it. I hypothesize that because professors are free to teach whatever they wish; in a free country, they have something called academic freedom. That the freedom to present the truth of what Lincoln said is, well, a violation of their freedom, I think.

I was working with Scott and Ivan today. Administration had set our table right in-between the Socialists and the Capitalism Sucks tables. Whether this was supposed to be funny or a test of our ability to get along, I am not sure. We talked and laughed, and then the crush of students for the Fall Student Club involvement began. My job would be to shout out above the crowds, "Free markets, free minds, individual responsibility, and self-reliance! If this is you, this is the club for you." I would shout this for the next four hours.

SICK

"The real man smiles in trouble, gathers strength from distress, and grows brave by reflection. The harder the conflict, the more glorious the triumph. The world is my country, all mankind are my brother, and to do good is my religion."

—Thomas Paine

After days and weeks of working student involvement fairs, my throat and body gave out. Early in the morning—1:00 a.m. to be exact— my throat flared up. Almost like strep throat, but without the fever and shakes. I worked to get my body back in balance and began heavy drinking. No, not that kind—water. I downed vitamin drinks and elixirs, gargled, and kept moving. By the end of the day I had staved off what I had feared was a pounding and debilitating migraine. I had just wrapped up and completed three straight days of out-of-town travel—University of Penn in Philly, Urines College. By evening I was feeling better and ready to keep going on to the next—University Kutztown—but before I left Philadelphia I had to meet a fellow patriot, Tim and his wife Kristen, at the Reading Market. I never know if when you're sick you should cancel appointment or not. Understandably, some people do not want to be around you when you're sick. I took a risk, sucked it up, drugged myself up with Robitussin, and went.

Tim was a fellow political writer and a retired military man. He brought his granddaughter, who had just finished her master's degree and was looking for some sort of work that would fulfill her, give her meaning. She had thought about becoming a cop, but because of the recent execution of cops, decided that because she had a son it was probably not a good time right now. The Reading Market in Philadelphia is a converted train station that now serves as an indoor market of food and beautiful chaos. Lots of Philly police eat there, so I felt at home, given my previous profession. Anyway, we talked about her experience in a Catholic university class taught by a Marxist teacher who had tattoos all over his arms and a shock of purple hair in front. She said that he told them that if they did not write positive things about the Atheist Karl Marx, he would downgrade you. I think there is a sickness in this country right now that a simple spoon of Robitussin will not fix. It will take a generation to cleanse this youth of the poison it has been fed. Our food arrived and we joined hands. We all said a prayer that day for more than our lunch.

TO KNOW AMERICA, IS TO KNOW BENJAMIN FRANKLIN

"The scriptures assure me we will not be examined on what we believed but what we did."

—Benjamin Franklin

Once Benjamin Franklin's newspapers became successful, he turned his attention to serving the people of Philadelphia, perhaps influenced by his father, a protestant minister. Benjamin began to focus on improving the lives of ordinary citizens. His genius was in forming groups of people to address social needs and not to depend on government to do so. He put together associations, a volunteer fire department, lending library, a society to exchange medical information, and found ways to get the streets paved and lighted. The new world would lead the way in discovering ways to make life better for ordinary people. And of course, education. He founded the University of Pennsylvania in Philadelphia, its first university, and here I stood, right smack dab in the middle of it, staring at a statue of the man himself.

How perfect and appropriate then, that I was meeting with the newspaper, *The Statesman*. There were three students and myself, all manning the table. Today was University of Pennsylvania's student involvement fair. Tables as far as the eye could see ran down the sidewalk, all presenting the various clubs students could join. The crowds were crushing; I could not believe how many students were at just this one college!

As the students came by, we handed out pamphlets or took sign ups. Some wanted to engage in conversation. One young guy stopped by the booth and did not like that we were mostly a conservative-based newspaper, and so wanted start a fight. I don't blame youth. That is why old men do not fight wars—soldiers are young and want to test their wit and weapons. And so he began at me, "You know the founders had slaves, don't you?" I am not sure where he was going with this, and so I replied, "So?"

He said, "Well, that proves America is evil and was based on the tyranny and oppression by the white man." Now in this situation, if you're smart, you only have one option, and that is to squash him like a bug. It makes no sense to point out to him the long history of man's inhumanity to man of all races, or that slavery was the mental furniture of the time, and for half the population to attempt to wrestle that idea from the other half of the population would have caused a war. America happened to be embroiled in the Revolutionary War already. A wise strategy is to just fight one war at a time. But for me to explain this would be too much for his already over-indoctrinated brain, so I simply said, "It's true, some of our founders had slaves, they also had indentured servants. I can tell your family probably came from that lineage." He looked at me with daggers in his eyes, until his friend carried him off and they were swept away in the crowd, never to be seen or heard from again.

I made it in late to an Airbnb. The sun was just going down and I had the house to myself. A three-story home, it looked to be at least a hundred years old. It did not seem creepy in the day light, but when darkness came, it took on a creepy atmosphere and lost its charm. I was to go up a long dark set of narrow stairs. There were three stories, each level a little creepier than the other. I spent the night on the sofa by the front door that night with my eyes wide open.

In the morning, I noticed a letter on the table that I had not before. The owner of the house introduced herself as a newly-hired urban renewal advisor. She bought the house to be involved in her new job and hoped that we would enjoy staying there. She had bikes downstairs to ride and food in the refrigerator, and hoped that everyone that stayed there would recommend the home and the area to their friends in order to revive this little piece of neglected Pennsylvania. It was a thoughtful note and very sincere.

I left early for Ursinus College. It was to be another student involvement fair. Zacharias Ursinus was a 16th century Catholic theologian from Heidelberg, Germany. I am helping the Libertarians today. When I get to their table, it is all set up with a theme I am not too happy about—legalizing pot. It's not that I want government involved or not, it's just that I think these kids should get high on life. It's much more interesting. As the students come by one after the other, I thoroughly enjoy their thought, banter and enthusiasm for the future—this is what I like most about my job. One vibrant young woman came up. Blonde and with the biggest smile, she was a philosophy major, and we connected well. I was so engaged in conversation that I forgot what I was supposed to be doing, and I think about ten people got ignored. Oops.

I got to my next Airbnb earlier today. The host and I had agreed that I should get the key from around the house by the chicken coop and let myself in, as she would be home late. I grabbed my bags, opened the door, headed down the hallway, and settled on the bed with my laptop and began documenting and logging in the day's events. About four hours later and nearly nine o'clock at night, I heard the front door close. *Did this person work as some kind of shift worker to keep these hours?* I thought to myself. I walked down the hall, and there in the kitchen was a slender woman about my age, but looking very tired and not just worn out from the day, but life. "Hi," I said, "I am Suzanne."

"Hello, my name is Debbie, so nice to meet you, would you like some tea?" We sat at the kitchen table and talked like old girlfriends. She told me that her job as a teacher was very difficult because of the internet. Some days she would have to spend the whole lesson plan unteaching the students all the misinformation they had gotten from the internet the night before. She taught seventh grade science and had stayed late to grade papers. She looked forward to retirement.

Usually when I am with a person for the first time I listen intently to what they do for a living, and what their hobbies and interests are. Since I had been at the University of Pennsylvania— Ben Franklin's college— earlier and knew his love of science, I began talking to her about his interest in electricity. As I yammered on about how awesome Benjamin was, I looked over and noticed that she had fallen asleep with her head resting in her hand.

THE LANDLORD

"What we obtain too cheap, we esteem too lightly."

—Thomas Paine

My apartment sits two blocks from a major railroad track, and I was made aware of this my first night around 2:00 in the morning by the loud blast of its horn. I thought, *Great, I found a place right next to a major industrial thoroughfare! This is either going to be quaint or obnoxious for the next few months.* But then came another loud siren, this one sounding like an air raid horn followed by fire engine sirens. I got up and looked out the window just in time to see the tops of their light bars whizzing past the fence in front of the courtyard. The next morning when Benjamin came up to bring me a table I asked him, "What are all those sirens and horns?"

"Oh Gawde," Benjamin says with his thick Jewish accent, "I went to City Hall once and asked if there was not a noise ordinance, and I was taken aside by the mayor of Mechanicsburg who told me, 'Benjamin , keep it down, that train siren is a tradition. Every time the train goes by the siren goes off to warn the hobos who sleep along the train track to wake up and to move.'" Benjamin looks me right in the eyeball and says, "Can you believe this guy? When was the last time America had a hobo problem? But then he finally tells me it's a tradition, and you don't mess with people's traditions."

Benjamin was clearly ticked off, but I was not even referring to the train noise or train whistle noise, but that third noise; that loud air raid siren. Somedays you would hear it, and others you would not, so it could not be to announce the hours of the day. So what the hell was it? After further pushing and probing on my part, and much to Benjamin 's agitation, he finally answered about the third deafening noise. "Oh, that one. That is to call the volunteer firefighters any time there is an accident. I think that one is dumb, too."

This conversation either proves that people are only listening to you about fifteen percent of the time and are consumed with their own agendas eighty-five percent of the time, constantly seeking, figuring and listening for ideas that line up with their cognitive bias, concerns, or frustrations. Or it could prove that he had become deaf because of the sirens.

I think Thomas Paine must have been a frustrated landlord when he wrote, "What we obtain too cheap, we esteem too lightly." For weeks now, Benjamin has further agitated me by having covert inspections under different white lies. "Oh I'm having a cleaning lady up on every Wednesday." When Thursday rolled around and it was quite evident that no "cleaning" had taken place, I became irritated. Not that he was protecting his property, but that he was lying about it. I thought, just come out and say you are inspecting it. Nope, each week would bring forth a new story. "I'm having a person come and spray, fix the electrical, and evaluate the paint color."

It was becoming ridiculous, so I began to beat him to the punch. "Hey Benjamin , you might want to come up here and check out this tear in the carpet; Benjamin , you might want to come up here and check out this chip in the paint; Benjamin , you might want to check out this toilet it is not flushing fast enough." I knew if I played the part of the overly concerned and needy tenant, his concerns over the condition of his property would be satiated. It worked, and the "inspections" stopped.

After some time, Benjamin and I settled into a respect for one another, and after a few more conversations over the weeks we began to talk more and more about politics. He was a retired college professor who taught of all things leadership, so was interested in what I did exactly. He told me that Israel was socialist and many European countries were successful at it. I told him that they could keep their socialism, for only the sake of giving people of this world a choice.

Far too many people forget that America in 1776 was the great experiment, that up to that point the world order was a people that served government and not that a government should serve the people. The idea that a people could govern themselves without interference from bureaucratic order was revolutionary. This new idea attracted political scientists from all over the world—people like Alexis de Tocqueville who wrote *Democracy in America* in 1835, who thought socialism was not a very good idea simply because it is the antithesis of human flourishing. Dispirited souls who are given everything they want and need would become lethargic and incapable of perceiving, much less acting on the freedom, responsibility, and dignity both inherent and unique to the human condition. After I point this out to Benjamin , he does admit that since coming to America he has made more money in ten years than he did in the thirty he lived in Israel.

PHILLADELPHIA

"If we will not be governed by God, we must be governed by tyrants."

—William Penn

October 27, 1682. William Penn named his new city Philadelphia by combining two Greek words, *phileo* for Love and *adelphos* for brother, resulting it the endearing nickname, City of Brotherly Love. As a Quaker, Penn had experienced religious persecution and wanted his colony to be a place where anyone could worship freely. I remind myself of this as I drive past so much rich history—the giant cathedral churches, statues, and bridges. When I had first entered Pennsylvania, my head used to snap, aghast at such architectural beauty. Now I had to stay focused on jay walkers, beggars standing in a street divide that jammed their coin cups at my window, bicycles weaving in and out of cars, and buses like giant mastodons, pushing their way past all of us. I had an appointment with a club at Temple University. It wasn't the best part of town, and I was wide awake and paying attention to any little thing that would pose as a threat, so this took a huge amount of concentration. By the time I got to the college, I was already spent. My meeting lasted only an hour, and then I had to decide what to do next. The Rocky Statue was nearby at the Philadelphia Museum of art. I could make it over there if I just had a chance to collect myself. After about a half hour of some deep breathing, a bathroom break, and rehydrating, I did some deep knee bends, stretched, and got in the car and took off.

I parked the car in an underground garage, which cost another five hundred dollars. Nah, just kidding; but it does cost a lot to park in the city. I started out looking for the Rocky Statue. After about an hour I discovered it. Then I ran down the stairs and had a couple of girls take a picture of me in front of it. I realized I needed to run up the stairs just like in the movie, so went back up the stairs, handed my phone to another tourist, and did the Rocky victory dance at the top of the stairs. Then I went over to a short wall and just sat and stared and breathed it in. Yes, I was a silly California tourist. The locals don't do this, but I was a teenager when the movie was made and remember watching it with my then boyfriend. The movie meant victory, overcoming odds, and being young. Seeing the statue reminded me of those messages, and so I just sat, looked, and remembered.

Once I was done being silly, I began to discover the museum—the cultural heart of the great city. Like Philadelphia's own Parthenon, the museum sits majestically at the end of Benjamin Franklin Parkway. As the third largest museum in the United States, its holdings are impressive, with exhibits featuring the work of Cezanne, Rogier van der Weyden, and Philadelphia's own Thomas Eakins.

What caught my interest were the statues outside, in particular a statue of Mary Dyer. She left England and settled in Boston in 1635 when the colony was a Puritan theocracy. She converted to Quakerism in the 1650s, and soon after the New England colonies established the laws banning Quakers. Exiled from Boston, Dyer was resolute in her commitment to Quakerism and its ideas. She repeatedly defied the unjust law, and was hanged in 1660, becoming a martyr for religious freedom. The principle of separation of church and state is a direct result of her death.

DIFFICULTIES DISAPPEAR

"I expect to pass through this world but once. Any good there-fore that I can do, or any kindness or abilities that I can show to any fellow creature, let me do it now. Let me not defer it or neglect it, for I shall not pass this way again."

—William Penn

I have lived long enough to come full circle with the same personalities I know I have met before in some other job, place, or circumstance. Like some sort of déjà vu, this person with a different name but the same personality is brought before me again and again. It is my wish as a fallible human being that any mistakes I made in the care and handling of this sort of person in the past is not repeated. My hope is that I somehow remember the lessons of yesterday and perform better on the day I am challenged again. I was challenged again today at a little university by the name of Kutztown.

Her name was Katie, about twenty-six years old, overweight, long brown hair, and a really big mouth—loud, but smiling. As we stood by our small table of limited government materials, she did a great job working the passersby. She was selling it. "Hey, how are you?" she would ask. "Hey, do you think Big Government sucks?" If yes, she would lure them in with swag, buttons, mugs, pens, bottle openers, posters, and books. She was working the crowd like a real saleswoman, and I did not have a problem with that. The problem was, it made me feel like she was raking her nails on a chalkboard. That it was all insincere; her conversations and movements with everyone, including me, were tactics and not traits. She moved with a deliberate effort to endear herself to people so that she could get her way, and people fell for it.

I had learned something in Jujitsu years ago, and that was when someone charges you with force, do not meet force with force. Simply be aware of it and step out of the way. And so I did. She saw a conversation taking place between me and a student, and I saw her lumber over. I knew she was going to step in between us, but I did not realize this would be executed so excellently. As she made her move, she thrust her hip towards me to shove me out of the way. Counting on the resistance from my body to stabilize her, she made her move, but I moved and she fell onto the grass. "Oh my goodness, Katie, are you okay?" I put out a hand and she got up, and dusted herself off.

"Yeah, I guess so. Not sure what happened, guess I lost my footing!" I nodded and shrugged.

I knew it would be the last afternoon we would work together. Did she change? Nope. I am sure of it. But did I change? Absolutely. In my younger years I would have gone for her jugular and we would have had a scream fest, me in my outrage and her in order to protect her ego. I had learned to not sweat the small stuff. Somewhere along her life journey she would learn, but for today, all she had was a sore butt.

GETTYSBURG

"I must insist on being spared the inflictions of such truism in the guise of opinions as you have recently honored me with, particularly as they were not asked for."

—General George Meade, Oct. 1863

Saturday—my day off. It took me longer than expected to get over to Gettysburg township and take a tour. Even though my children had been grown for quite some time, I still feel thrilled every time I order one ticket, buy one sandwich, and pack only one backpack to get on a bus and take a tour unhindered by the demands of others. The freedom and excitement it brought me made me smile every time.

The tour guide was great, pointing out bullet holes on the sides of buildings still there today, and the homes of families that sheltered soldiers as they came marching and fighting through the once-peaceful township. Since there was no radio or phone, the battle that spilled onto their streets was a complete shock. The people were conducting business as if it were any other day; there was no warning that this was about to be the bloodiest battle of the Civil War right there on their front door steps.

The bus made several stops for us to get out, and at one point I noticed that there was a short, roundish, middle-aged man in our group dressed up in a Confederate uniform complete with hat. I hid behind a cannon and watched him. I watched as he asked the tour guide questions, and then got back on the bus. This person was different from the rest of us, so the next stop, I went up to him and said, "Gee, I notice you have on a uniform, tell me about it." He turned, stood upright like a small, fat owl, and began to chirp away.

"Oh yeah, I'm a Civil War buff, and I have learned so much about the war, and you should too. Lincoln was really an evil man, and very self-interested in his own agenda. He was a liar and a manipulator, so many people do not know the real Lincoln. But I watched a good documentary, and I learned the truth. The name of the documentary was *The Real Lincoln: A New Look at His Agenda and an Unnecessary War*, By Thomas DiLorenzo"

I kept my mouth closed, smiled, and nodded. He was clearly convinced of his revisionist history and not about to budge. Not wanting to make a scene, I politely bowed out. But the encounter did make me realize something unique about the tour. The guide never really did say one side was right and the other wrong. The material was laid out matter-of-factly, as if both sides had a good point. I found this completely wrong, only because it was a testimony to the times—that people today only believe in personal truth, that it is elusive and cannot be found. This is dangerous thinking for a country.

At the end of the tour there was another author, a Mr. David Dixon, who was sitting in the gift shop quietly selling his book, *Gettysburg, The Lost Address*. We talked about this man dressed in Confederate uniform. Although I had just met Mr. Dixon, we both agreed that the book the Confederate soldier was so enamored with was simply a product of someone, who would write anything just to say he had written a book. Mr. Dixon and I agreed that people need to understand that published does not mean true.

BERNIE AN UPDATE FROM THE WAR FRONT

"Those who want to reap the benefits of the great nation must bear the fatigue of supporting it."

—Thomas Paine

September 12, 2016. I left Mechanicsburg in the morning and headed out later than I wanted to. Phone calls and emails went out, but I was not sure that they went anywhere. It was probably 10:30 by the time I headed out. It takes over three hours to get to Pittsburgh. With stops etc., around four hours. Late in the morning I had arrived in Pittsburg. The tough thing about being in a new area is the work/mission thing combined with the sightseeing thing. Looking and driving at 40 miles an hour while watching for pedestrian, unfamiliar lane turns, and your stopping point can be kind of dangerous. As your neck snaps and you put your eyes back in your head, you find that you have nearly missed a head-on collision. This all happened when I passed the Phipps Conservatory and Botanical Gardens. If you have never seen it, it's like a giant opulent terrarium surrounded by a sea of green grass. By day's end, the newspaper I had started was doing well, the students had invited good speakers to the university, and we organized our next activism event, which was handing out Constitutions in order to get people to actually read them. I had one last meeting. I plugged into my required conference call, sat in my car, and looked longingly at the conservatory, which would be closed by the end of this meeting.

The sun was just setting as I pulled into the Airbnb I rented. I choose which Airbnbs I will stay at based on a picture of the host, cost, and reviews. This one had a picture of a cute younger college looking gal, and I liked the young, so you would think I would have had enough of them during the day, but no, they have an optimism about them, since life is new. I texted her and asked her how long to get there. She texts back: *oh only 6 minutes!* That was the beginning of the lies! It took me over 30 minutes through driving hell—foreign and awkward intersections with no clear delineations. People familiar with them seemed to be driving 80 miles an hour, pushing me to make up my mind quickly, and if I chose wrong I would suffer the consequences. "Fuck you!" A blast from their horn. Over bridges, through tunnels, and over pot holes the size and depth of the Grand Canyon. Thoroughly rattled, I pulled up in front of the house. It looked like a model meth lab home from the pages of some sort of upscale drug magazine, *Better Homes and Boozers*. I am not happy. I call this time and do not text. A man's voice, lethargic and indifferent, answers. "Yeah, what do you want?"

I left. I was on the phone with Airbnb, letting them know of the misrepresentation. They were good, and about two hours later I had my money back. I drove for miles not knowing what to do. The sun had set, and it was near impossible to navigate foreign roads now. I found a high place, Point of View Park right near the Point of View statue—a sculpture in bronze by James West. It depicts George Washington and the Seneca leader Guyasuta with their weapons down in a face-to-face meeting in October, 1770. It was very cool, but one more thing I did not have time for. It did, however, seem fitting that all three of us were experiencing the unknown.

As I reclined my car seat and settled down for a long winter's nap, I was awoken by my phone ringing. "Hi, its Airbnb. We found you another place," the lady said. I forced myself to move, not really sure if it was worth it at this point, but I looked at the clock and it was only eight in the evening, so I went. About fifteen minutes later I drove up to a cute home, with a cute gal at the front door and her front yard littered with "Go Bernie" signs and "Socialism is Awesome." I dealt with it and went to bed.

TIMES THAT TRY MEN'S SOULS

"Either write something worth reading or do something worth writing."

—Ben Franklin

I can't write anymore because my computer is not working. It is my computer's turn to be sick. Although I love being a private contractor and having my freedom, it has its drawbacks. I cannot just go to the office and get another computer. This whole endeavor has to be me; I, am the only one that I have to rely on. I got to get this thing fixed, and fast. Lost time is lost opportunity is lost money. I looked for a Staples. I love Staples. For fifty dollars a year, it's like having a tech savvy family member anywhere in the U.S. I went in and put on my cutest girl whiny face until I got a guy by the name of, wouldn't you know it? Krishna. No relation to Hare. I was there all morning. He checked it. Virus scan—1 hour. Then come back and decide what to do. Renew virus protection reinstalled—1 hour. Peace of mind—priceless. But the day was half over. Blah, okay. Panera Bread for the remainder of daylight. Send out emails, make phone calls and a broth bowl.

Today I met Kevin from another freedom fighter group. We set up a table together and quickly found out we were from the same tribe—raised with Christianity and limited government, individual responsibility, and self-reliance. We fit well together despite our thirty-one-year age difference. He was an interesting fellow, graduated from Scranton Pennsylvania as Valedictorian, accepted an internship at a political think tank, finished his internship, and then kicked out into the big mean cruel world where he met me and this difficult job.

It was a slow day. There weren't a lot of students out today, so we had the opportunity to talk. Well, he talked and I listened, because frankly I was sick of my own story.

He says to me, "You know I ran in the Boston Marathon the day the radical Muslims set the pressure cooker bomb off."

"What the heck, are you kidding me?"

He went on. "Yep, I crossed the finish line and a few minutes later it went off. In fact, in some photos of the news story you can see my parents and sister in the background. It makes me shake to the core each time I think of it or see those pictures, thinking how narrowly we missed being killed or maimed. You know after it happened we were all in a daze, hundreds of us. But my family, I remember specifically finding them in the crowd and not knowing what to do. So, we all just wandered and walked. We walked right into a seedy side of town where my mom finally broke the silence and says in a meek little voice, "Do you think we are safe here?"

I just lost it at that point and started screaming. "For God's sakes woman! We were just bombed, are you fucking kidding me? And you want to know if we are safe here on this side of town? Jesus H. Christ!" I just kept screaming like a maniac until I realized I was losing it and starting a whole other scene. I had totally disrespected my mom, so I shut up.

He said he quit running after that and went back home to just breathe. He is now back out in the world and wondering where he fits in, just like I feel often in my life. I told him that I envy people who have a linear life—they know exactly what they want to do. Not so with folks like us. Life seems to be like a raging river set with stones across it that we must test for stability. Some stones are wobbly, like jobs, and not to be trusted. Some stones, like the jobs we take, are wobbly and not to be trusted. Some stones break under pressure, and some are solid and offer a place of respite, but know you cannot rest there long before being swallowed up the raging river. If nothing else, Kevin and I certainly had things to write about. I knew that I would write about Kevin and our friendship. I also knew I would have him as a friend for the rest of my life. He was a person of good value.

GOVERNMENT PROTECTED SEX

> *"We are all born ignorant, but one must work hard to remain stupid."*
>
> —Ben Franklin

I t's late in the evening. I completed another long day's-worth of work, and have to enter it all into my database. I need Wi-Fi like I need water, so I settle into a cute little restaurant and begin. I went cheap today—a thirty dollar-a-night Airbnb and a teeny-tiny bed that was propped up high. There was a small ladder to climb into this bed, and it turns out it was this man's ten-year-old son's bed that he rented out on the days his ex-wife had the kid. I was spending two days in this area, and so two nights at my host's house. On our first night getting to know each other, he divulged to me that he had gotten a divorce from his wife because he decided he was a bi-sexual, and she did not like that, and she did not think it was good for their marriage. Makes sense to me.

I then told him what I do for a living—push for smaller government and fiscal responsibility. If people want to be socially liberal, that is up to them and not for government to legislate it. The thinking is this: if government is involved in parts of your life that you want it to be, it will most certainly be involved in parts of your life you do not want it to be. So better to let people figure it out themselves, and for government to just stick with the basics. In the words of Thomas Jefferson,

> *"A government big enough to give you everything you want is also big enough to take away everything you have."*

Eric was a webpage designer, and we discussed my web site. He said it looked amateurish. I agreed, and he said that he would help me fix it. So this encounter was turning out well. We continued to talk for the rest of the hour right up till bedtime. He told me he was from Vietnam and had moved here when he was ten years old with his mom. He loved America because, as he said to me while sitting on the couch, "People in America leave you alone to do what you want. "I told him that many people who are homosexual are libertarian because they do not believe that anyone should dictate to them how to live or where to live or what business they should practice. It was the concept of being free in a free country that appealed to them most. Again, small government. I don't think Eric understood this concept, because after we discussed him revising my website, I got a call two days later, rescinding the offer to rebuild it. In his text to me he said:

> "Suzanne, after looking at your website and your Facebook page I find that I cannot commit to redesigning it. If you remember we discussed how some people are at different ends of the pendulum than others, and this is the case with us. I cannot bring myself to fully embrace redesigning your work, as it is opposite to my ideologies. Eric."

I guess that's the end of that. I suppose I could sue him like the cupcake, the photography, and the florist people all got sued for not providing services to people they disagreed with. I was certainly being discriminated against because I was a heterosexual. The thought of how ironic and ridiculous the world had become struck me at that moment.

SOMALIA

"The happy Union of these States is a wonder; their Constitution a miracle; their example the hope of Liberty throughout the world"

—James Madison

I drove across the top of Pennsylvania today on my way down the state to meet up with Kevin at West Chester University. With mile upon mile of hills, trees, and valleys, it seemed my eye could see till the end of forever. I cranked up my radio to Neil Diamond's *America. We've been traveling far without a home, but not without a star...* I was the happiest I had been in many years, free to be me, free to be just, well, free. I was like a wild woman as I sang the lyrics at the top of my voice. I put all the windows down. My hair was in my face and the colors I had heard so much about were right there all over the mountains. Orange, yellow, vibrant green. It was glorious. In the words of Abraham, "A man is as happy as he makes up his mind to be." I had made up my mind to be pretty damn happy.

The days had settled into a routine. We knew what to do, what to say, and what to hand out for each conversation we had. But today was a little different, because a woman from Somalia came up to our table, and she said she loved our table. The conversation began; she was fascinating. She said people in America are ridiculously lazy. They want something for nothing. She is so happy to work, and she does work—two children, two jobs, and college classes. She says that when she tells her family back n in Somalia all about America they think she has died and gone to heaven.

She says no, that she still must work, but then they respond that they too would be willing to work twice as hard if they could only have the opportunity to come to America. They tell her they would be so happy just to work here and never complain. We finish listening to her, and know she is correct, and wish that people that hate America could hear her, but I think those that hate America probably make a good living demonizing this country through their speaking and writing. Still, I wish I could somehow find a way to amplify her voice.

DON'T GET YOUR PANTIES IN A TWIST

"True friendship is a plant of slow growth, and must undergo and withstand the shocks of adversity before it is entitled to the appellation."

—George Washington

I tabled at Millersville all week and got a club started. This was so huge for me, and exciting. Ron Paul came to talk on the third day at Gettysburg, so I headed over there just to hear the great one talk on limited government. I got there late because I had another fight with my GPS, who led me 20 miles away. Ron Paul graduated from Gettysburg and got married there. He spoke with great conviction and unwavering principle. He was consistent. At the end of his talk he took questions from a few in the audience. Inspired by his life story, some shared their shared passion and interest in running for political office, but to my surprise, he discouraged them. He said, "If you want to help the world, the best way to do it is without bureaucratic intervention. People who demand money out of you and demand you abandon your principles is not the best way to go; the best way to change the world is to change people one at a time." I found his message both irritating and honest.

Throughout the whole presentation, my phone kept ringing that I had a text. I had a guy named Mark texting me. *Where are you? I'm here, where will you be at the end of the presentation?* We had accidentally met up on a Facebook page. There was a group of locals who were carpooling to the Ron Paul event. I had begun interacting with these people, but then decided not to carpool because of my work schedule. This guy Mark obviously took a shine to me and started in for the kill. At the end of the presentation I met Mark. He immediately asked me out to coffee. The night was young and I wouldn't mind adult conversation, so I accepted. We drove our cars over to the Lincoln Café on main street, sat down, and ordered coffee.

Turns out he was a lonely divorcee. Says he went to West Point and did some years in the army, but got out because of bad knees. His weight showed his lack of activity. I told him about my years as a peace officer, and he began telling me about the time he went into Wal-Mart with his gun under his shorts. The bulge showed and alarmed a woman who came up to him and said, "Did you bring a gun in this store, sir? Is that a gun in your shorts, sir?" He said he looked at her and said, "Well, I think that is kind of a personal question lady, so I will make you a deal. I'll show you my gun if you show me your panties!" Mark let out a blast of laughter like a harbor seal, which got the attention of people around us. I made an excuse to get the hell out of there quick. "Well, Mark, I gotta go. As you know, I am working and I have a lot of ground to cover, plus on the weekends I have to see as much as Pennsylvania as possible before I go back to California."

He said to me, "Where are you going this weekend?"

I knew as soon as I opened my mouth that I should not open my mouth, but one of my biggest faults is honesty. I cannot lie. Believe me, I have tried, and I always get found out. "Falling Water," I stammered.

Mark jumped on it, "Oh, I would love to go, I have never been."

I did not think much of it. I squirmed my way out of the restaurant, into my car, and out of Gettysburg.

Two days later, my phone rings. I look down. It's a text from Mark.

Mark: *so when are you going?*

Me: *oh, about 1:30, if you want tickets you have to call*

Mark: *done*

Me: Nothing. Oh dear Lord, what have I gotten myself into? I just sit there and hold the phone in my hand. I knew this was just the beginning of this guy.

It had been a long few days. I pulled into the Tarzan Hut driveway, got out of the car, grabbed my backpack, and opened the courtyard fence. As the gate swings open, it pulls the laundry line in front of my face, and I must duck under the line. Sometimes I get smacked in the face with laundry and must duck quick. Today it was tiny lace panties strung along next to Benjamin's big white boxer shorts. The thought of them rolling around in bed together was, well, this is the end of this journal entry. That's all I got to say about that.

TIMES THEY ARE A CHANGING

"We have too many high-sounding words, and too few actions that correspond with them."

—Abigail Adams

A text today from my youngest daughter. Her very first child is born, a son, and my very first grandbaby. People congratulate me and say, "Oh, you're a grandma now, how do you feel?" I think the question is stupid because it is not about me. I feel the weight and responsibility of what it means to fight for the freedoms our grandparents have all had to. Freedom from over regulation and bureaucratic tyranny is every generation's responsibility; I feel the weight of responsibility just a little more today. I know one thing about being a grandma. I will be a grandma that tells my grandkids to live like I and their mother did. To suck it up; life is hard, but it is adversity that will be your strength and advantage.

This youngest daughter of mine is an incredible human being, and I believe a product of this mindset of mine. She graduated high school, served her country in the Air Force, graduated with a Master's degree, turned around and started her professorship at a University, married, started a family, and is finishing her black belt in Jujitsu. She was always go, go, go since she was a baby. Some of the students I meet in my university travels remind me of her. She and they never expected anything, but worked for it. They did not resent it, but relished in the rewards that hard work brought.

There is another grandma getting a lot of attention today—Grandma Hillary. She is visiting a nearby convention center today, so Kevin and I decide to go and listen before going to our next university. She speaks today of what the government owes other people; that we Americans need to be given more; that the country is unfair and a vote for her would make it more fair. She is a grandma that I sense will enable her grandchildren, and offer a crutch to those that do not want to work for what comes to them, thereby robbing them of the growth, satisfaction and strength that comes from hard work. Kennedy, a great Democrat, said, "Ask not what your country can do for you, but what you can do for your country." I think there is some incongruity between these two Democratic messages.

There are two mindsets in this world: one of scarcity, and one of abundance. A scarcity mindset says that there is not enough, so I must take and hoard. The abundance mindset says that this is enough, and if there is not enough I will make more pie or a bigger one. I have always believed that if you live your life with an abundance mindset, people will reach for more, create more, and share more. But that is where America is divided today—these two trains of thought: one of scarcity and one of abundance

I was reading a poll that said that this was the most divisive election that anyone can remember. People were reporting to have lost at least one friend due to the vicious, passionate differences of opinions and sides. There are those who say this election will forever change the direction of the United States, never to return to anything remotely looking like what the founders had envisioned.

HERSHEY—IT'S NOT ABOUT THE CHOCOLATE

"Individual Ambitions Serves the Common Good."

—Adam Smith

It's the weekend, and I have been kind of dragging my feet about going to the city of Hershey. it seemed that it might be overrated. Only 30 minutes away from me, I got up Saturday morning and headed over there. As I entered the town, the amusement park and giant Hershey smoke stacks rose above the horizon. At first look, it seemed that Willy Wonka, Walt Disney and William Randolph Hurst had all had a head-on collision here at this intersection.

I drove up to the highest hill past an arboretum, a school, and up to the opulent hotel. I parked my car and looked out over the empire—the amusement park, the factory, Chocolate Land, a zoo, and off in the distance his city, complete with local theater and coliseum for the hockey team (the Bears) and of course the city of Hershey. But it was not until I got into the museum and began to relive his life story that I was taken aback by his complete immersion and acceptance into the beauty, power, and moral reasoning behind the free markets as the founders had envisioned it. A man left to his own devices, equipped with self-reliance, determination, and a strong dose of good towards his common man could create such a massive difference in the lives of other people.

The hilarious thing about Milton's story is that his success was by accident. On a trip to Europe he was shocked to see people eating his chocolate-covered caramels. They would bite into them, spit out the caramel, and devour the chocolate. He decided to go back to America, sell his caramel factory, and focus on chocolate.

There are some strong parallels between Milton and Andrew Carnegie. Both had absent fathers and strong mothers that instilled in them an appreciation for hard work. Both had failures and successes, but persevered because of that work ethic. They both had a passion for education and philanthropy, both giving back everything they ever made to their communities, all without a government organizing or controlling it. Milton's creative engines had been personally inspired, released, and set free in the free market completely without bureaucratic order making it so. Here was another story of another great Pennsylvanian and an American. I had no idea.

ASSHOLES, POWER, AND MONEY

"When people fear the government, there is tyranny; when the government fears the people, there is liberty."

—Thomas Jefferson

I walked in some of the most extravagant university buildings in the world, more opulent than even the great buildings of Europe I had seen thirty years ago. Universities are big businesses, and it is because there are government subsidies for education. For example, imagine there were no public subsidies for education and people and parents paid for their own children's schooling. Individuals would shop around for the best and most competitive price, whomever offered the most for the least would get their business. Now, if there were no government guaranteed student loans for college, do you honestly think that parents would or could pay fifty, sixty thousand dollars for college? Not likely, because schools would not be in business long, due to the fact that no one could afford it. There is an arms race among colleges to gain customers, and because of this, each university is spending massive amounts of money to attract more customers, uh, excuse me, students, i.e. dollars.

I was headed to Haverford today to meet Kevin and a man running for a local political office, and then to the University of Haverford. I think about all the driving and think, *well, two hours is not so bad, but then it depends how many assholes you meet on the road.* At one point, I was first up at an intersection. Mind you, all intersections are foreign to this California girl. And this jerk honks his horn on a red light, as if to say, "Go, stupid." And I think, *where, asshole? Where the hell do you want me to go? Into the intersection?*

These people just honk. I think they drive with only one hand; the other is hovering constantly over the horn that is not a horn, it is a "fuck you" device that they are addicted to— a constant pay-it-forward. Someone honked at me, now I am going to honk at you, and keep this chain of being uncivilized going on and on. I think of a bumper sticker I could make that would start a movement. It would say, "Honk Back." Then every time one person honked, every other single person honked, drowning out *their* honk, making them realize that it was stupid to honk in the first place because no one could hear it. Well, I think about this kind of stuff when I am driving and tired.

Doug was running for supervisor and wanted to meet with us. I'm not sure why; maybe just to network, but Kevin asked me if we could before we went to the next university, so I said yes. Doug came out of his office and gave me one of those hand/triceps arm shakes and shook my arm until I felt it start to come out of its socket. He was sort of a Chris Kristy type of fellow, only without the charm. Kevin and I introduced ourselves as Kevin and Suzanne. He immediately shortened our names to Kev and Suze. Each time I tried to start a conversation, he would increase his volume and walk right over me and Kev. Kevin kicked me under the table, which meant it was time to go, and we were off again to the next campus. It was Kevin's idea to clipboard in the cafeteria. I said we should walk the walkways, but nooooo! We got about 20 signatures before a campus cop came up to me and did this little tap, tap, tap on my shoulder. "Huh? Kevin, we have to go." As we were escorted out, I saw a table of mean girls, glaring at us with phones in their hands; they had called on us. You know, the kind you remember from high school? They have that look—smug, snobby and vindictive. Funny how no matter how old you get you still want to just yank their hair.

We went on to the next college where we met up with one of my club leaders, Jay. We made plans and gave him supplies, packed up, and called it a day. I was thinking about the three-hour drive home when Kevin says to me, "Stay in the area another night and we can hit a lot more colleges in this same area tomorrow." Well, I think to myself, if he had an idea and a plan I was game; only thing was that I was not prepared, so I had to go and rebuy all my cosmetics and tooth brush and some pajamas. I found an Airbnb, and late in the evening met up with my latest host Cornelia, who lived in Ardmore. I knocked on the door and was met by an older, smallish woman from the Philippines with a very big smile. As the door swung open I was hit with the smell of her fabulous cooking.

With a big happy voice, she says, "Oh, drive to the back of the house. I have a private room for you," waving and pointing the whole time. It was a nice, private room. She showed me the Internet password and says she is embarrassed that it is so long—G2KF56K5FSMLYNL5. She is right, and I think, *are ya kidding me?*

I settle in for the night and put my head down. Then my phone rings—it's a text from Mark.

Mark: *so are you having a good week?*

Me, four hours later: *yes I am, I am meeting several interesting people.*

Mark: 3 hours later: *I am not meeting interesting people*

Mark: *looks like we are going to have an interesting weekend* He sends me a picture of hurricane Matthew.

Me: *Yes*

Cornelia calls me upstairs in the morning and has on a huge breakfast spread. A retired nurse and the only one at home, she clearly loves the company. Loneliness is the number one problem of the elderly. They are often drugged up or suffer great depression because of it. The Airbnb system has been a Godsend to these people. On a fixed income they are able to make some extra money and also get exposed to people and conversation—something the human soul craves.

THE SHIFT

"A man wrapped up in himself makes a very small bundle."

—Ben Franklin

Sundays I clean, research, and get ready for the following week. The job can be overwhelming at times, and I remind myself to take one step at a time on the days that it does. I do my laundry at a laundromat. I have not done that since I was a newlywed in my early twenties. Only thing that is different now is that you can put a movie on your laptop while you fold laundry. I had on a movie called *The Shift* by Wayne Dyer; it was his desire that everyone on the planet watch it. Its message was about what true happiness is, and it was very familiar to me. Countless motivational speakers had this message, and there were at least twenty-five Bible passages I could think of that had the same message. If you want a truly fulfilling life, one filled with happiness, then put others before yourself, and ask people more often, "How can I serve you?"

Ironically enough, earlier in the day I had picked up the *New York Times,* which had an article about new legislation being proposed to restrict Airbnbs, and earlier in the week in Texas to restrict Uber drivers. According to Dyer and Jesus, it is an essential human need to serve others. Not only are the middle class earning a little extra pocket change, but they are creating and maintaining a civilized society by being afforded the ability to serve. The brilliance of these systems is not in earning the money, it is in the morality of system and its ability to enhance a community.

These two new industries have given people the ability to be human to each other and to serve one another through the traditional free enterprise system, each getting what they need from the other—a place to stay for the night, getting a ride, and the dignity of earning money through your own efforts. A shift is possible from service of self to service towards others.

I fold the last of my towels and my phone rings. It's a text. I look down, its Mark.

Mark: *Hey have you heard of the band Madison Rising?*

Me: *Yes I have they are called America's most patriotic band, but I am not so sure, my husband's band The Sierra Mountain band is more patriotic, you should check out their web site* www.SierraMountainBand.com."

Mark: No response

THE GREAT WORLD'S FAIRS

"The eyes of the world being thus on our Country, it is put the more on its good behavior, and under the greater obligation also, to do justice to the Tree of Liberty by an exhibition of the fine fruits we gather from it."

—James Madison

Kevin is driving today, and we are on our way to the universities in and around Philadelphia, but since Kevin is driving and not me, he has taken me on a route I had not seen. He takes me past some of the most incredible statues. He drives past them like they are nothing at fifty miles an hour. My eyes linger on them until my neck snaps back into place. "Slow down!" I yell at Kevin, like he is one of my kids. "What is this place?"

"Oh, this?" He says it like it is nothing. "This is the International Sculpture Garden, and it's run by the Fairmont Park Association. Along with newer pieces, many were put in to celebrate the first official World's Fair and to celebrate the 100th anniversary of the signing of the Declaration of Independence back in 1876. Nearly 10 million people came from thirty-seven countries, just to see it."

"Oh, is that all?" I say.

There are just too many to list—over two hundred—but the ones I see at break neck speed are a statue of Saint George slaying the dragon, a Muse leading a Pegasus, the incredible Gettysburg Memorial Arch and the last: Lenni-Lenapi Indian Chief. He knew every twist and turn and corner. We were flying past things I had only read about. If it were not for him driving as erratically as a squirrel looking for nuts, I might have enjoyed it more. But he was an excellent tour guide, since this was his childhood playground. He told me about how it had become forgotten and dilapidated over the past decade, but there was a revival and a re-building that was slowly taking place again.

Then he pointed out something fascinating and odd. "Look at the street on the right, there are only black people walking on the side-walk. Now look at the left side; there are only white people walking. It's self-segregation. I think people just like to be with people they can relate to, and it's as simple as that. Too many people jump to conclusions, when I think it just has to do with being around people you're comfortable with." It made sense to me.

We set up our table on this warm, sunny fall day, happy to be spread-ing joy and liberty to anyone to talk about it or wanted a book on eco-nomics, or just a copy of the Constitution. We talked to students about being masters of their own destiny, in charge of their own lives and the money they earn to have the joy of giving it away like Milton Hershey. Or we would simple ask people, "Who is going to make the best decision for you? The government, me, or you?" Usually when I phrase it that way, they get what smaller government means.

But today I was confronted by an older man whose mind was like concrete, all mixed up and set. He looks at me with condescending look. "So what's this, some Right Wing thing?"

I said, "No, we are just trying to bring attention to the founding ideas of limited government and fiscal responsibility."

He kept at me and asked me suspiciously with his eyebrows fur-rowed, "So are you with Grover Norquist?"

What? I think to myself. I looked at him and cocked my head like a small puppy hearing a strange sound for the first time. It worked. He cooled his jets. "You don't know what I am talking about, do you?"

"Uh, no," I said. "Look, we are just trying to bring attention to a cou-ple of financial issues and the Constitution so these ideas don't get for-gotten about, kind of like World Fairs, no one really hears about those anymore, do they?"

"Oh, okay," he says and walks off.

I look at my partner. "And that's a wrap, Kevin. Let's head home."

FUNNY SEEING YOU HERE

*"Nothing is more essential to the establishment of manners in
a State than that all persons employed in places of power and
trust must be men of unexceptionable characters."*

—Samuel Adams

A trip to Philadelphia from Harrisburg and Mechanicsburg always
forces me onto the Pennsylvania Turnpike; it is a road you pay for.
As a Californian, I have never experienced such highway robbery, and
if I were a local Pennsylvanian I am sure I could find my way around it
and still get where I wanted to, but am not, and at the mercy of the GPS
who tells me what to do these days. When arriving back into town from
Philadelphia, the GPS always dumps me back through the same turnpike
gate with the same woman at the toll booth, I am not kidding you. I have
tried to use different gates to get different toll booth workers, but oddly
enough, there is Irene, no matter which gate I enter.

"Hi Honey, how are you tonight?" We chat and begin a kind of funny
1-minute banter relationship. Tonight it's 8:00 by the time I get into Mechanicsburg. I test my theory that each time this woman sees me coming
she screws with me and goes running under some underground tunnel
to the booth that she sees me driving to. I slow down and choose a gate I
have not tried before—the far end.

"Hey, girlfriend, how are you doing?" I'll be damned, its Irene again.
"Oh," I say, "Today I was caught at one of those weird Philadelphia intersections that the locals seem to know so well, and I got honked at and
yelled at, and one woman threw her arms up at me, as if to say I was an
idiot. I started shouting back, and then threw my arms back up at her.
Like, how in the hell am I supposed to know about all these sneaky little

side lanes? This woman who had a honking melt down on me—I can just imagine her whole life she was probably a huge fuck-up, and here is this one shining moment when another woman, me, is fucking up more than her. She desperately wants to point this out to the world, as if to say, 'Here she is world, honk, honk, the stupidest woman in the world, honk, honk, point, wave, point. And it's not me, world!"

Irene and I laughed and laughed. She was black and I was white. Contrary to current media propaganda, there was no racial tension with her or anyone else I experienced or witnessed during my months of being here. We enjoyed our brief encounters making fun of the crazy world and sharing stories.

Irene says, "Oh, I hear you! I love Mechanicsburg. The people are calmer, the roads are nice and wide, peaceful shopping. And you know I moved over here from Philly, for a boyfriend, you know, but whatever! So, after I left his sorry ass I had to figure my way around and I just got lost, you know what I mean? I just got lost, but during the daylight you know and I figured it out. You will too, darling."

"I hear ya; I'm trying," I said. "Well, nice talking to you, Irene; see you next time around."

"You take care, honey, and be safe! "

"You too, Irene!" I yelled back as I drove away.

We really like each other and would probably hang out if time allowed. I think to myself, *racism is kept alive by race hustlers, and people who get a sense of superiority by denouncing others as racist. I wish they would stop, the world would be so much nicer if they would just shut the fuck up.*

I got into bed late again that night, dog tired. My phone rang. It was a text.

Mark: *Hey, is this you causing trouble?* He sends a picture of speech ball.

Me: *no, that is not my group but, yes that's what we do*

Mark: *oh, I thought so. I was wondering if you want to drive together to Falling Water on Sunday?*

Oh Gawde, he just will not let go. The more polite I am, the more he keeps pushing it. How in the hell do I make him get the message? Maybe if I accept then I could talk to him and tell him face-to-face that I am happily married and not interested in him. No, that is a stupid idea. Oh, wait, I'm booked at an Airbnb for two nights the day before. *That's it. I'll tell him the truth. I will not need to drive together since I will already be in the area. He won't believe me and he will have hurt feelings. I have to do it. Just text it, Suzanne! Okay, here goes.* (Two hours later)

Me: *Hey Mark, sorry for the delay, I used my phone as my GPS and was on the road and had a million people texting me. Uh, oh well, um here's the thing. Unfortunately, I am already booked in that area so will not be commuting from Mechanicsburg."*

Mark: *well I cannot justify driving solo for four hours over there, and I have a really big day on Monday*

Me, to myself: *This son of a bitch had no interest in seeing Falling Water!*

I know, I know. All you savvy dating women reading this right now knew this long before I did.

PRIVATE SECTOR, PUBLIC SECTOR AND NON-PROFITS

"The prosperity of commerce is now perceived and acknowledged by all enlightened statesmen to be the most useful as well as the most productive source of national wealth, and has accordingly become a primary object of its political cares."

—Alexander Hamilton

October. Autumn. Colors on the leaves are even more vibrant with reds, yellows and oranges. Many leaves are beginning to fall and blow across the highway like snowflakes. I am a little less than halfway through my assignment, and a melancholy has set in for me. I think fall makes many people feel that way—a time of reflection on what the summer brought, and putting it all away; the lawn chairs, the umbrellas, and the summer toys. Time to brace for what comes next—winter. Chopping wood and preparing for the long cold darkness, this could be a depressing thought if one thought about it too long, so I won't, and pushed it aside. The interesting thing about life is that humans seem to need the clear delineation lines that seasons bring. Too often we move from one event to the other in a fog and don't take time out to celebrate goals reached. I was very fortunate to have reached my work goals and the required numbers early on, which gave me the time I so desperately needed to write, think, and research what to do in this next great adventure called life.

I have worked for the public sector, government, and the private sector in real estate. This was a first, working for a non-profit. The way money is obtained, flowed, spent and invested is very different for all three, and I am baffled how any normal person can vote for economic policies unless they have a clear understanding of all three sectors. The only people creating wealth is the private sector—those people inventing or making things, such as iPhones, cars, or Krispy Kreme donuts, and those that are service-oriented, such as janitorial services, in-home care, or auto repair, to name a few. The government and nonprofits get money for what they need and want by forcibly taxing, or in the case of nonprofits, begging. There was a time public workers acted as a support system. They got paid less than the private sector—the wealth creators—that has now flipped. According to a San Francisco paper, a university in San Francisco chancellor by the name of Sam Hawgood makes $651,100.00 annually.

The only reason this non-profit I work for now emerged was because of how this dynamic changed—from the servant to the master. Public sector universities voraciously demand money from the public while keeping out the public, creating fiefdoms of thought control rather than places of balanced and critical thought.

FALLING WATER

"Architecture is my delight"

—Thomas Jefferson

As I turn into the next university parking lot, my phone rings, it's a text,

Mark: *Hey I am going to pull the plug on that trip to Falling Water and get my money back within the 48 hours, have fun.*

Oh, there is a God.

The weekend I had been wanting to see Falling Water. I arrived, and although I had been struggling with weekend loneliness from time to time, this was one time I relished being alone. Frank Lloyd Wright's creation had captivated me since my early college days when I took a few architecture classes. It was built over the Bear Run River for the Kauffman family as a summer home, and is listed on Smithsonian's Life List as of one of the 28 places to visit before you die.

It was not exactly a good day for me to drive there. The rain was heavy, and the three-hour drive would be long. I drove through rain cells, fog, and past 18-wheelers so determined to run small cars off the road that every now and then, little Jesus on my rosary would do a flip around the rearview mirror. I kept saying to myself, "Ten and two, ten and two, scan the road, three car lengths, ten and two." Just then a ginormous swarm of blackbirds flew high overhead, headed straight into another one, and then quickly diverted direction in a split second, creating a beautiful fireworks pattern of organized chaos. I slowed to watch, but not enough to get a horn blast from an 18-wheeler. I had learned my lesson in Philly.

I left Falling Water and headed to my next Airbnb. Jeff greeted me (I was only 15 minutes late, not bad) and his wife Alice was not going to meet us because she was in her room passing a gallstone. He told me he had passed one last month, and it was her turn now. "Oh," I said. What do you say to that? I could not imagine. So I said the standard, "Oh, I am so sorry to hear that." We sat on the sofa and chatted, he with one eye on me and one eye on the widescreen TV with a football game on. He told me he was a senior day care provider, and helped the elderly with things they no longer could, like bill paying and grocery shopping. His wife was a teacher and taught seniors in high school. I noticed a small baby scooter in the corner of the room.

I said, "Grandchildren?" He got a little silent. "Well, yes and no. This last week was the baby's one-year anniversary of his death. He passed away at eight months old." He told me to check out the Facebook page the family had created for him, "A Life of Smiles." He said there were videos that his family had put up and he had never watched them until yesterday. He went on.

"I thought I was ready to see them, but then realized when I started watching them, I was not. "It's still hard."

What do you say to that? That's something I could imagine, as I thought of my brand-new grandchild, Joshua.

The subject changed nearing dinner time. I asked for his suggestion for a local restaurant. "Oh, the Primanti Bros, we just got one here in town and you won't be disappointed." I knew I had heard that name before in Pittsburgh, so I yelped it again, the review read:

"What is more Pennsylvanian than Primanti Bros? Seriously, I feel like we should kick you out of the state if you're not into it. Of course, Primanti's also gets to brag the highest number of sweat suits per capita in the tristate are, but who cares about looking fashionable when you can get a heap of French fries on your sandwich and salad. God Bless America!"

I thought to myself, no wonder you two have gallstones! "Um, how about something smaller?" I asked. I settled on a tapas restaurant he recommended. Thirty dollars later, I came through the door to meet Alice sitting on the couch in her sweat suit, blanket wrapped about her, and a laptop propped on her lap. We both began chatting immediately. She was warm and friendly, but had opinions about things, so I shifted to listening mode as much as I could. When she asked me a question, I did my best to answer it in a not-too-serious manner. She asked me what I liked or noticed about Pennsylvania since visiting here. "Well," I began, "I noticed that when I drove through Amish country that the roads have not been designed to accommodate the horse and buggy, and since they have been in Pennsylvania since the 1600s, William Penn and religious persecution and all, that they would have accommodated them. Apparently, the horse and buggy vs. car accidents are pretty bad."

Alice thinks about this and says, "Well, they are really rude people." Now I am thinking to myself, *Wha? What does that have to do with the price of eggs in Yugoslavia?* I could have chalked it up to her being in a bad mood because of her gallstone, but figured it was more a part of her normal everyday personality.

Point of View statue in Pittsburg, Guyasuta, a Seneca leader, and George Washington. In different times and different ways, these two men had a great impact over events in the region.

Valley Forge, George Washington, a leader who taught us how to be strong and how to learn and grow from adversity.

Victory and overcoming odds: Me with Rocky in front of the Philadelphia Museum of Art.

The Town of Jim Thorpe formerly known as Mauch Chunk.

My dear young friend Kevin.

HOSPITABLE VS. INHOSPITABLE

"Work as if you were to live 100 Years, Pray as if you were to die To-morrow."

—Benjamin Franklin

It was to be an inhospitable afternoon. I had a meeting with one of my group leaders today, and so I figured I would set up at a table with my usual books on economics, copies of the Constitution, and paper in case anyone wanted to join the club we had or create a new one. I have always prided myself on exceptional displays of eye catching arraignments. This time it caught the eye of the wrong person—a campus cop. Since I had done his very same job in a previous life, I knew intimately both his mind set and his plan of action. One—he could listen to reason how free speech is protected under the First Amendment on a public campus. Or two—he could do the opposite and be a mindless bureaucrat, and only do what he is ordered to do, which is remove any person from campus that is not promoting the same ideologies as the campus. My money was on option number two. Yep, here he comes. Long story short, I am asked to leave. The last time I had a female cop and explained to her, she liked the positive message and left me alone; even took one of my stickers and slapped it on the back of her patrol car. But if I know anything, (and I know cops) this guy was an ignoramus, and probably was just thinking about his next paycheck and how he was bothered by someone to get up and do something. I was the cause of his consternation, and so he would remove me. I could push it and risk getting arrested, or yield and find another way. I yielded and packed up only to live to fight another day and move to another campus.

Winter is trying to push fall out of the way. Although I sit in a sunny bright spot outside the campus café, cold is seeping past my clothes and into my bones. But I stay at my post like a sentry on guard duty. I am what I am, and I am not leaving until I have engaged some students in freedom-loving conversation and met with my student leader. Four hours later, I gave directions to someone on where the bathroom was, talked to an Arab student on economics, and ate my sandwich. At the very last hour, I met with my student. I was packing up and a girl approached me. College students are inquisitive, and that is what I love most about them.

She noticed I had sat there for hours, and that I had a few books with me. We began discussing what I do, and she asked to interview me for the school paper and publish a "how to get in contact." I think the thing I love about this job is that you never know what is going to happen each day, and the thing I hate about this job is that you never know what is going to happen each day.

Around dinner time I met a most hospitable host at this Greek restaurant I had been passing for weeks. I had lived in Greece on the island of Crete for three years and remembered well the gyros I was so addicted to when I was pregnant with my first. I was sure the price would be different—back then they were sixty cents.

I ordered the gyro with lamb, and it was very chewy; not the tender meat I remembered. I was not too happy, and so filled out a suggestion slip. I was about to put it in the box when the owner stops me and says, "What's the problem?" almost panic stricken. I tell him, and he says I ordered the wrong meat. He takes my hand and drags me to the kitchen and makes me another one, this time with pork, but does not stop there. He keeps the food coming—fries, tzatziki sauce, Greek salad, another kind of meat, and on and on. I was so focused on the food that I forgot about Greek hospitality. They will feed you until you pop. My mouth stuffed full like a chipmunk, he fills a paper bag with more food, hands it to me, slaps me on the back, and tells me to come back and tell him what I think, then.

MA'AM

"The dons, the bashaws, the grandees, the patricians, the sachems, the nabobs, call them by what names you please, sigh and groan and fret, and sometimes stamp and foam and curse, but all in vain. The decree is gone forth, and it cannot be recalled, that a more equal liberty than has prevailed in other parts of the earth must be established in America."

—John Adams

I am a Zig Ziglar junkie. If I just hear his voice, that man can put a smile on my face. For those of you not lucky enough to know who he is, he was a motivational speaker who had a southern drawl and had mastered the art of the pause. I even made my kids listen to him on the way back from the grocery store or soccer practice. Zig coined the phrase, "Your attitude will determine your altitude." But today did not start out well, and the rest of it remains to be seen. It started when I got to the Subaru service counter, and the guy says, "What can I do for you?"

With a big good morning on my face I say, "Hi, there! Well, I need one of those six thousand, sixteen thousand new cars tighten up your bolts service thingies."

He says, "Ma'am." I knew it was not going to come out well. Whenever someone completely dismisses your cute perkiness, pushes it aside, and says, "Ma'am," it is not going to go well. "We do not have a six thousand, twelve thousand tighten up your bolts things. Now what can I help you with?" I stand back as if I have just been shoved.

"Well, um, I am from California and I have a newer Subaru. I drove all the way over here and I think it needs the fifteen-thousand-mile checkup." He continues to ask me what I want, and I cannot express it any better than I already have. I don't speak Subaru.

This little squirrelly guy next to him decides to have a crack at me, and says, "Ma'am, we don't have a six thousand, twelve thousand tune up the bolts thing." Oh, my Gawde! I scream to myself. *I am being facetious, not literal, okay?* I think I am just going to sit down. I left and went into the waiting room. I knew they would seek me out after they got their heads out of their asses. The squirrely guy did first, and began again. We both took a deep breath as he talked. We eventually get settled on the Subaru fifteen-thousand-mile checkup. A half an hour later I am out the door with an oil change, tires rotated, and a washed car. That's the fifteen-thousand-mile checkup? That's it?? Well, okay.

I have a 4:00 appointment with some students, and I figure I will just table all afternoon up till my appointment. I get to Elizabethtown and am discouraged to discover that it's a private college! *Shit!* It's locked up like a fortress—no right to free speech here. The day is half over, now what? I will go to a coffee shop and re-strategize. I get to the car, and halfway there to the coffee shop, the GPS screen goes blurry. No service. I am lost. I cannot go forward and I cannot go back. So, I decide to park at the McDonalds and regroup. I sit down and notice I must have landed in Oakey Ville. Everyone in this restaurant looks like they have come right of the movie *Deliverance*. One guy catches my eye; he keeps staring at me, and every now and then he would yell at his kid, "Reemund, git over heau."

The little boy had to have been three years old, but could not talk much. I began to think the situation looked a lot like a kidnapping case I remembered from my cop days. I decided to call the local police and have them do a welfare check on this kid to make sure the man with him is legitimate. The guy grabs up his kid, throws him in the truck, and I write down the license number. The dispatcher transfers me to another local police department. Then they send me to a different dispatcher with a bad connection. "Ma'am? Who are you, ma'am? Ma'am, I cannot hear you. Ma'am, if you would just repeat yourself, ma'am. Yes, I heard that, ma'am!" Oh my Gawde, there have been too many withdrawals today from my patience bank! I finally get through to her, and that was it. A cop calls me ten minutes later and says that I have only given the dispatcher six numbers and not the seven necessary to run a complete license plate check. But the cop says to me, "Ma'am, if you see the guy again, ask him for the complete license plate number and call me back."

What? I breath out loud. *Dear God please let it get better.*

I sit back down, center myself, take a deep breath, and begin to type. I look down at my hands and think they look old. When did I go from being a miss to a ma'am? My hands, once smooth, now have deep lines and pronounced veins and knuckles. I begin to doubt myself. Who in the world would ever believe I am a transfer student on these campuses when I look so old? I begin to withdraw inward and start just hating everything and feel my once positive upbeat attitude of this morning going into the toilet fast. Zig, where are you when I need you? Then a group of about 15 senior citizens decides to sit next to me. They could have chosen the whole freaking McDonalds, but no, they gotta plunk down right next to me. "Whatcha doing? Gosh that is an awfully big mouse you got there, looks like a rat!" I get up and leave. I decide that I will just wait in my car for my 4:00 appointment that will only last 10 minutes. That's it. Ten minutes of work today with some students who won't appreciate me or the tremendous value of what I have to offer them. I just keep repeating in my mind over and over, *your attitude will determine your altitude.*

ON CUTICLES AND COMMUNISTS

"Experience hath shewn, that even under the best forms of government those entrusted with power have, in time, and by slow operations, perverted it into tyranny."

—Thomas Jefferson

I had vowed to make this day better. There was a light rain, so it kept people mostly inside. If they did walk by my table, it was quickly as they ducked into the nearest building. One young man walks past my table promoting free markets and limited government and says, "Communism rocks!" I do not let it bother me. Kevin joined me today, and I was grateful not to be alone, but he began to complain about the futility of this job; that the assignment was so abstract that you never knew what was going to happen each day; how each morning he wanted to quit. I agreed, and that is what friends do. They listen, but always offer some sort of motivation or encouragement. His complaining sparked a memory from *Lord of the Rings* When Gandalph talks to Frodo, who is fed up with his assignment to save the world; that it was so abstract that he never knew what was going to happen each day, and every morning he wanted to quit. He was sick of carting the stupid ring around. So I look at Kevin and say, "Remember that movie *Lord of the Rings*? And…when Frodo says to Gandalf,"

"I wish the ring had never come to me, I wish none of this had happened."

Gandalph replies, "So do all who live to see such times, but that is not for them to decide. All you have to decide, is to decide what to do with the time that is given to you."

"You know, Kevin," I said, "that is the turning point of the movie, when Frodo becomes convicted in his mission and begins again, inspired and renewed by this truth." Kevin was only briefly inspired by my passionate reenactment of this movie scene, but only briefly, and certainly not as much as I. Oh well. I tried. I thought it was brilliant. I had never read the book by J.R.R. Tolkien, but I read his biography and knew that *Lord of the Rings* had been inspired by the events of the second world war, more specifically power-grabbing tyrants. Tolkien knew as all people who live through power grabs that the struggle is always started under the guise of "doing good."

As I drove home my index finger began to throb. A broken nail was now splitting and bleeding because I had let it go too long. I stopped at a very small nail business about a block from where I was staying and walked in. There was only one Vietnamese man and his wife there, and I asked if they could fix me up quickly, and the custom response, "sure, sure, sure, have a seat," was his reply. With a nail tech, it takes a few moments to get the conversation going. Minh, which means brightness in Vietnamese, lived up to his name. As he took my hand we began to talk. I love conversational people, so this was going to be pleasant for me! He did have a thick Vietnamese accent, though, so I had to work hard to listen. We decided I needed all new nails, and it was going to take longer, so I asked him to tell me his life story. Age has taught me that if more people would just put a sock in it and listen, they could learn some really valuable lessons in life. This is what I learned that incredible afternoon.

Mihn's story was as follows.

"After the Americans left Vietnam, the Vietcong swept in, imprisoning and punishing Vietnamese that cooperated with the Americans. Some, like my father, who had used his three-story bakery to feed the Americans, and my sister who interpreted for the Americans, were given asylum out of the country. My mother and the rest of my nine brothers and sisters were left behind. My oldest sister went to America and my father to Malaysia. Before he was forced to leave, he told my mother to sell everything and get out of the country. And then the Communists swept in. They tore apart the bakery, took everything, and left a giant hole in the side of the wall of the building, then told my mother that government regulations required her to fix it immediately. My brothers and sisters all scattered. Some were arrested and some made it to Germany and Australia. My mother ended up in Germany with one of my brothers, but I ended up in prison for nine years! I kept escaping and they would throw me back in. The last time I escaped I was out for a long time; long enough to get married and have a child before they caught me and threw me back in again.

"There are different levels of Communism, like Russian Communism, but Korean and Chinese, those are the worst. In this prison you must grow your own food or die. They also have no heart; Russian Communist will shoot a whole bunch of you and throw you in the ground. The others—Chinese and Korean Communist—will just throw all of you in a hole and bury you alive!"

As he choked up, I could see this walk down memory lane was not easy for him, and I questioned the wisdom and kindness of letting him continue. I did not want to let him relive the suffering, but I knew this valuable story must be told, if even for a few paragraphs so that people could learn from it, and so I let him continue.

"A prison guard came to me one day and said we have to let you go. the American Embassy has said we must, and so you are free. My sister who was in America had been working for my release for nine years. That is how I got to come to America, but she could not get it for my wife and daughter. So, when I get here, they get me a job at a donut shop because I know bakery, and I also took a second job at a fabric dye factory. I worked so hard to forget my loneliness. I worked all the time so I do not go crazy because I miss my family so much. But after two years of working hard and saving ten-thousand dollars, I was able to go back to Vietnam and see my family! My daughter, she was now two-and-a-half years old, and of course she had no idea who I was. I stayed for a month, and the whole time she was distant from me until the day my wife took me to the airport. She finally hugged me and said, 'Daddy, do you have to leave?' I began to cry. I cried so hard that I could not leave, so I did not get on the plane and stayed two more months. But when I got back to America, of course I had lost both my jobs. That is when a friend told me I needed a profession and not a job, so I studied how to do professional nails. I went to school and studied by day, worked at night, and took English classes so that I could speak to my customers. I love my work."

Rarely silent, I was at that moment, hearing his story. It was not that I had not seen movies or read books about such things, but it was because right here and right now he was holding my hand. As I looked down at his hand, and felt the warmth of it, I thought about those fingers which had traveled through so many years of work and heartache across so many miles. I felt every word of his painful and joyful journey.

It was not until nine years later that he would be able to legally unite his family and bring his wife and daughter to America. His son came two years later. He has been running this very successful shop here with a charming yellow facade in downtown Mechanicsburg for nineteen years and has quite an impressive clientele list. I won't ruin the rest of his story for you because I told him he needs to write a book, and his daughter, now a doctor, has told him she would help him do so.

Interestingly and unfortunately, his battle continued with big government here in this land of the supposed free. The town wanted to him to move his nail shop because it did not fit with their vision for Main Street, which was to be wine shops and art studios. Those in power wanted to ignore such facts as people's right to property and to commerce freely unobstructed by over regulation and excessive restrictions. He eventually won that battle too, and likened local government to a bunch of Communists as well. He is right, and he is an incredible human being.

When I go to college campuses I wish I could drag Mihn around with me and shove him in professors faces, and put him on a soap box in the Quad of every campus and tell his story. The biggest question is not why the young are people fascinated with Communism and big government, but why professors teach and encourage it. That is the question for this century.

BOOKS ALL AROUND BUT NO INTELLEGENCE

"The good Education of Youth has been esteemed by wise Men in all Ages, as the surest Foundation of the Happiness both of private Families and of Common-wealths. Almost all Governments have therefore made it a principal Object of their Attention, to establish and endow with proper Revenues, such Seminaries of Learning, as might supply the succeeding Age with Men qualified to serve the Publick with Honour to themselves, and to their Country."

—Benjamin Franklin

A mid-sized community college. I set up a table with my little books about economic freedom and personal liberty, Adam Smith's *The Wealth of Nations*, and the free market. I put out a small American flag, pulled out my phone and lunch, and sat in a sunny spot, prepared for a lovely day in the sun and stimulating conversation. I texted Kevin for moral support, since each day it is difficult when you are alone to motivate yourself to get out of the car and fight a battle alone. However, Kevin needed the moral support.

Suzanne: *hey Kevin, not really into this, this Monday morning*

Kevin: *hey, me neither, I did not even want to get out of bed, got to love this job!*

Suzanne: *well, when I am having a tough day getting motivated like this, I treat it like a picnic! I have my lunch and my phone and I sit in a comfortable spot and if the people come up to me and engage fine, if no, I have still met my obligation and had a nice picnic and kept my morale up!*

Kevin: *that sounds so pleasant when you phrase it like that.*

The funny thing about moral support is often when you go looking for it from others, it is others who need it from you. And like all spiritual advisors have ever preached—Wayne Dyer, *The Shift*—it is in giving that we receive, and so I gave Kevin the moral support and found myself feeling better for it as well.

A few people came up to my table and engaged me. On slow days like this, many that approach you are either dejected or lonely. Karen, a middle-aged black woman, came up to my table, and I think she was a combination of lonely and curious. She had a voracious learning appetite, and I will never forget her. She immediately began on economics and told me she did not know anything. I told her there are two economic systems for the most part— one is a socialist system and the other is a free market system, and that is where people get confused, because the media confuses it. But you have to ask yourself only one question, "Which system is the most moral to the most amount of people?" As long as you send all questions through this filter, you will have your most moral answer.

She begged for more, so I gave her another five points and a pile of books and some videos to watch. She was over the moon and told me I had taught her more in that ten minutes than she had ever learned in all the years of school. She said I should be a motivational speaker. That was a good one.

The second was the dejected one. I think more than being dejected, he was dropped on his head as a small child. He comes right up to me all tatted up and constantly looking over his shoulder at some invisible pursuer. He says to me, "Yes, I am for limited government and I am for socialism, and I think Karl Marx had it right!" Okay, where do you begin with that? I let him continue. "You know the Catholic church was invented by government, because in the Bible it says, 'Give to Caesar what is Caesar's.' Right there it tells you the Catholics are the government."

I began, "Well, it seems to me you have given this all considerable thought. Here is a free book, have a nice life."

KARATE VS. KARAZY

*"Men, in a word, must necessarily be controlled either by a
power within them, or by a power without them; either by the
Word of God or by the strong arm of man; either by the Bible
or by the bayonet."*

—Robert Winthrop, Speaker of the U. S. House

Today I got attacked by an "intellectual." He came flying from around
the corner of a building, went straight up to me as I stood in front
of the recruitment table, stopped about twelve inches from me, pointed
his finger directly at my face, and shouted, "You should be ashamed of
yourself. This group is backed by the evil Koch brothers! You should be
ashamed of yourself." And then he turned to my young club member and
said, "You, I can forgive because you are younger." And then he turned
back to me and shouted again, "You I cannot forgive because you are
older and should know better." I thought to myself immediately, *gosh was
my undercover make-up and hair not good today? I thought I was pulling
off a pretty youthful me look, wow, that hurts.* Anyway, I got side tracked
in my thinking, but quickly regained my mental footing.

"Look, you want to attack the Koch brothers for supporting this
group, yet George Soros is the antithesis. He goes out of his way to promote the justification of government in business and the personal lives
of people with the excuse of global warming, when there are plenty of
scientists that have scientifically refuted it or its urgency. They have
questioned the vehicle of 'global warming,' used to push and justify population control and taxes on populations."

"That's a lie!" he screams back at me. "I am a scientist and I know
science, and there are no other scientists that refute global warming."
Angry and outraged, he took a step closer to me.

Now, I have to back up for a minute. The group that has called me to help them recruit members this lovely afternoon is called CFACT, which stands for Collegians for a Constructive Tomorrow. Their mission statement is:

1. ***Prospering Lives.*** *CFACT works to help people find better ways to provide for food, water, energy and other essential human services.*
2. ***Promoting Progress.*** *CFACT advocates the use of safe, affordable technologies and the pursuit of economic policies that reduce pollution and waste, and maximize the use of resources.*
3. ***Protecting the Earth.*** *CFACT helps protect the earth through wise stewardship of the land and its wildlife.*
4. ***Education.*** *CFACT educates various sectors of the public about important facts and practical solutions regarding environmental concerns.*

CFACT has a list of science advisors listed on their website, which I certainly did not remember. I wish I had at that moment so I could fire it back to him, but my mind went blank. I took a step back from Mr. Crazy, bladed my body in karate stance, and was prepared to dodge when he took a swipe at me, and fired back the only thing that came to my mind. "Oh yeah, well if you're so convinced that people are so evil and the cause of global warming, and that they need to be exterminated, why don't you go kill yourself and help out the environment? Just stop sucking up oxygen right now and help the environment!"

He took a step back, as if I had punched him! He stopped and said, "I can't believe you told me to go kill myself. I can't believe you told me to go kill myself." Stunned, and his feelings clearly hurt, he shuffled away taking a few looks back at me as he went off into the distance.

At this time, I wish to clarify some things about global warming to my readership. I have up to this point avoided labels for the simple reason that my wish for the universe is that people stop using them and think critically about issues without lumping them and people into a box of labels, i.e. conservative or liberal. It's disheartening when people throw a label at someone to shut them up—right winger, left winger, racist, homophobe, and on and on. The conversation is over, if it ever began, and there is no more exchange of information—only fighting. One would think that on a university campus surrounded by "intellects," those espousing higher thought would not be guilty of labeling people and things in a nanosecond. It was a learning day for me on this campus, and I did not even have to pay for the lesson.

HOST OR GUEST,
ITS ABOUT BEING GRACIOUS

"In selecting men for office, let principle be your guide. Regard not the particular sect or denomination of the candidate — look to his character..."

—Noah Webster

Before I left California, I set up my husband with an Airbnb account as a host. I knew he would be lonely and it would be good for him to host people. I just prayed he would not do old man things such as leave the toilet seat up and allow spiders to create homes in the corners of each room. He assured me it was all going well, and that each person was very happy. As I read the reviews from three thousand miles away, it looked as if he was in fact doing very well—he had rave reviews. And then that one review came in. I knew it was inevitable and here it was. "Caveat Emptor," the review read, buyer beware. I called him up and asked about the last guest, who would leave such and ungrateful review. He told me exactly who—a young socialist economist and her Russian husband. He went over the day's events with me.

"Everything was fine. They got here late and asked to watch the presidential debate between Donald and Hillary. They also asked if they could have free reign of the kitchen, so I let them. In fact, while they were cooking, I entertained the baby and played some tunes on my banjo. The baby loved it; she laughed and cooed at it, wanting to touch the strings. They sat down with their dinner and watched the presidential debate, that was it."

I never told my husband about the bad review. It would have hurt his feelings since he worked so hard to please people. But the review

84

detailed that what they did not like was the network he chose. They wanted MSNBC, and he had put it on FOX.

My dentist told me once he had worked on a Canadian's teeth, you know, the Canada with the free socialized medicine. He told me her teeth were all falling out and rotten, and she was only 26. He said it was because there is no incentive to do good work, and because you must wait your turn, he did not think in his doctor's humble opinion that socialized medicine was a good idea. There is no changing some people, but I am sure our Socialist guest thought that of my husband as well.

I am a guest today at an Airbnb in West Chester. Some people do not like hosting, and in this case, it was clearly her husband. The guest list of rules was long, and at the top was for guests to remove their shoes. She was great. She talked about being how she and her husband had come from India and she had been a housewife her whole life, but she did enjoy her alone time and took off often on the train to New York for Broadway shows and fine dining. She told me that Airbnb was one way she made extra money to do the things she wanted to, and driving as an Uber driver. But said that she was more selective as an Uber driver, since driving people around after four in the afternoon usually meant bars. Picking up people from bars usually meant cleaning throw up from the back of your car. Made sense to me.

That night I noticed that the guest toilet had a note taped to the back of the it. "Don't use a lot of paper." They clearly had a problem with their toilet and did not want to fix it, but to blame guests. So, following the instructions, I used like one square of paper. The next morning, I showered, used the toilet again, and packed. I was greeted downstairs by the dark stare of her husband. If eyes were daggers I would have been stabbed a million times over thrashing on the floor in a pool of blood. I wanted to be cordial, chat, and be friendly. As I accepted her coffee, her husband just kept staring at me. I smiled and began my normal chattiness, desperately searching through my brain files for a funny story that would appeal to an angry non-friendly Indian man. Safety experts say that people often freeze in emergency situations, not necessarily because they are afraid, but because they are encountering something for which they have no information on how to respond to it. Like a person caught in a plane crash for the first time would desperately think, *Okay, how did*

I get out of this the last time, or what was my training? Guess what? There are no memory banks to recall for this, because it is unlikely that you have been in a freaking airplane crash before!

Oh, gosh, what do I say? I think to myself after listening to the deadening silence for what seemed an eternity. He was just staring, staring, staring at me. My brain flashes to horses. "Oh, ah, yes. I had this horse who was so well-trained that it could make me coffee." I don't know why I said it. It was stupid, but I paused for effect.

He said, "How do horses make coffee?"

I said that they don't, and that it was a joke.

He said back to me, "I know. I was saying a joke, too."

This conversation seemed to irritate him even more. Words quickly poured out of my mouth. "Well, thank you for your lovely hospitality." I grabbed my bag, picked up my shoes, and jogged out the door in my socks.

"You can put your shoes on in the house now!" she yelled out the door to me.

"No thanks, I'm fine!" I yelled back as I felt the warm wet of a crushed snail ooze through my sock.

WINNER OR WHINER
YOU CHOOSE

"Success is to be measured not so much by the position that one has reached in life as by the obstacles which he has overcome."

—Booker T. Washington

As I drive through the countryside, there are political signs that remind me the country is in the middle of a great war. Each time I enter a city, the signs promoting a Democrat president are everywhere. "I am with her," they read. As I enter the country, I see signs for a Republican president everywhere—Make America Great Again. West Chester is not a large city, and has more Republican signs than Democrat signs. The quad in this university has an incredible castle, and in front stands a statue of Fredrick Douglas. He last spoke here on February 1, 1895. Douglas escaped slavery and became a leader in the abolitionist movement. He was a great orator, and helped moved the country past slavery. After Douglas's death, Booker T Washington took up the call to heal and to move forward. He was an educator, and played a significant role in reconstruction after slavery. He was a positive motivator for all races, and I happen to know his granddaughter. I had met her years ago while at a meeting for the National Speakers Association. She speaks motivationally as well, carrying on the message of her grandfather, Booker, who promoted healing and strength through self-reliance.

Today, Wednesday the 19th of October, 2016, the teachers went on strike. I didn't know exactly what to expect, but I had agreed to meet with Tyler, who had started a club called Students for Self Defense. We set up at 11:00 right by the food trough, otherwise known as Starbucks. We handed out pocket Constitutions, mints, and asked students if they knew of the campus policy regarding pepper spray, and if they could carry it to defend themselves. I wonder how many parents check out safety issues before they send their daughters to school? It's one thing for a campus to say they care about your child's safety, and an entirely different thing to do something about it. Although police deter crime by their presence, they obviously do not deter all crime, and cannot be at all places at all times.

As a security and safety expert, I am in my element today and loving it. I have a circle of gals around me, and I am showing them how to get out of wrist locks and arm bars. I'm teaching them awareness techniques and mindfulness tips to make them not only safe, but how to use those very same techniques for life success. I look up and discover I am drawing a crowd. No one cares about the chanting, striking teachers and how horrible life is for them. The students are gathering around me. I feel like Booker T. Washington. I am empowering and motivating right here in front of the food trough.

AN AFFAIR TO REMEMBER

"In all your Amours, you should prefer old Women to young ones. You call this a Paradox, and demand my Reasons. They are these..."

—Benjamin Franklin

Did you know that Benjamin Franklin was married? He was married to Deborah Read, and from all accounts, happily; but absently since he traveled a lot. Much is written about his womanizing, but I don't agree. From what I have read, he just loved the company of women, and one in particular—a Madame Brillion who was also married. I'll let you research that relationship on your own, but suffice to say that there is a certain thrill when someone takes a shine to you. It does not have to mean adultery, it simple can serve to only validate you; that you are still relevant.

I had not had my heart skip a beat like a teenager in many, many years until I entered that coffee shop at the end of that very long day. There were no other customers in the shop except this tall, good-looking man in a business suit at the counter who looked younger than me, but not by much. I walked into the "line" next to him and waited for him to place his order. He pondered the new hot chocolate—it sounded amazing—but he chose something else. So, when it was my turn I said, "I'll have what he's having, actually what he was going to have, but then did not have. Does that make sense?" and then looked up at him and smiled.

He said, "What's your name?"

I said, "It's Suzanne, and I only like special coffees, 'cause I'm special."

He looks at me and says, "I can tell you are special and unique." He then looks at the barista and says, "I am buying her coffee for her, she is very funny."

The barista looks at me and says, "What is your name?"

Then the guy says, "Didn't you hear her? Her name is Suzanne."

I said, "Yeah, that's my name." I looked at him and said, "What's your name?"

He said, "It's Jim."

"Jim," I said. I put my arm around his shoulder and said to the barista, "Meet my new best friend, Jim." Jim laughed again.

Jim went into the bathroom, and when he came out, his drink was ready. I said, "Here is your drink, Jim."

He said, "Thank you, Suzanne, it was great to get to know you, have a great day," and then he got in his car and sat there for about five minutes. What did that mean? Did he want me to go talk to him more? I was lonely on the weekends and would have loved to have had a friend, but then realized that it might not be a good idea. He was probably sitting in his car thinking the same thing. And so we sat there, me looking at him through the window of the coffee shop, and he looking at me through the window of his car. Finally, he drove away, us looking at each other the whole time, until his car drove out of sight.

My Airbnb was hosted by an older couple. My first couple host, they had been married for over forty years. The husband met me and led me up to another set up much like my Tarzan hut—a studio above a garage. The first thing I noticed was that nothing matched. I am such a matching snob sometimes, but unlike my temporary home, this had an artistic charm about it. A tapestry hung on a portable hanger closet for privacy, here was a small Ikea self-contained kitchen cabinet unit complete with sink, stove, and refrigerator. Her husband had made two tables out of saw horses, and all four corners had little lamps. There were plenty of wood framed windows to let in the light, and little notes everywhere about where towels were, where to eat, and how to turn on the coffee pot.

Some Airbnb hosts love their business and treat it like a real bed and breakfast, naming their facility. These people had named theirs the IMBY—the In My Back Yard at Misty Hollow, and had left little notes everywhere, like this one on the bed:

We here at the IMBY, Misty Hollow, provide you with 100% cotton percale sheets which are air and sun dried giving you a natural farm fresh scent as well as wrinkles. We hope you enjoy the freshness!

As I put the paper down and looked at my host, he said he had to get going and watch the debate. I said, "Who are you rooting for?"

"I'll tell ya one thing," he grumbles, "it ain't going to be that Trump!"

I wish people would stop thinking and voting for the person—Hillary, Trump, Hillary, Trump—and look more at the ideas of great economists like Fredrick Hayek. I wish they would do some research on which party follows his free market, and free people economic principles. I always tell people I am voting for Fredrick Hayek just to fuck with 'em.

My host asked me if I needed anything else, and then said he had to get going because tonight was his anniversary, and his wife had made a special dinner and was waiting for him. I told him that I didn't need anything, and decided not to watch the debate, but to write about the man in the coffee shop.

THE ART OF CONVERSATION

"The better part of one's life consists of his friendships…"

—Abraham Lincoln

My usual weekend routine again—church, gym, laundry, and the grocery store, all before I settled into my lonely apartment to research how to plan the coming work week. This week had been hard, as I was suffering from crushing loneliness. It's ironic that there would be so many lonely people in the world with so many people in it, especially in cities. I rarely had that problem because of my ability to reach out to people, but building lasting, deep relationships was a little more tough, because I knew I was going home in less than four weeks.

I had to get out and go talk to someone—anyone—and so I ventured out into the warm afternoon. I stopped at my local grocery store, picked up some things, picked out a cashier that looked chatty like me, and began. She was about twenty-five years old, five-foot four inches, and long blond hair. I'm thinking she weighed about two-hundred and twenty-three pounds. We both immediately engaged in what I call the lost art of conversation. I ask you a question, and then you respond. It's kind of like ping pong—you get a good volley going, and the momentum from a good conversation can be exhilarating. We were talking about the foods of Pennsylvania.

"Oh we love our beer, bagels, and cheese noodles here in Pennsylvania," she says to me with a gigantic smile. "And Tastykakes."

Now, that is something I had not heard of yet. I was very aware of the beer, bagels, and cheese noodles. The packages of cheese noodles seemed to be at the end of every isle in the store, and the smell of cheese noodles wafted from every deli counter. The beer section of the grocery store took up whole walls, while the wine section took up only a single row—a stark contrast from the wine prominence of California. The bagels are served at many local coffee shops and bed and breakfasts as a meal. Made with bleached white flour, my body screamed endometriosis every time I looked at one. But Tastykakes are not something I had heard of.

"Oh, please tell me what a Tastykake is," I said, not wanting to know what other variety of death by carbohydrate I had been missing. A deep voice shot out that had not been part of our intimate conversation.

"It's like a giant Twinkie," said the bag man. He was one of those informational types that don't have a clue about what is really going on—you know—the kind that cannot see you are making a human connection and not just looking for information. I did not honestly give a rat's ass what a Tastykake was, I wanted to have a conversation with this woman in front of me. He said it again, "Yeah, Tastykakes are like Twinkies, and if you want some, they are over there on aisle three."

I worked hard to keep my face from looking like I had been sucking on a pickle and said, "Thank you," took my things, and left.

One day I went into an Ulta store. That's where they sell a lot of overpriced make-up, and they make you feel beautiful because you have spent a lot of money on the same stuff you could have bought at Walmart. I needed my hair done today, so I asked the clerk where a good place to go was, and she said they had a salon in the back. I should have known better, but one-hundred and sixty-four dollars later I realized that I paid one hundred dollars more for the privilege of being in an Ulta store than I did at home, which would have cost me only sixty-four dollars. But the hair dresser, Katie, was a gem. She was sharp, educated, and quick to laugh. I felt like I was around my daughter, whom I missed so much. Being that I was lonely for people who I had a connection with, I went again six weeks later. I guess there is no price you can put on good conversation and a little friendship.

LOOK, LISTEN,
AND BE CAUTIOUS

"In the Fall of 1774 and winter of 1775, I was one of upwards of thirty, chiefly mechanics, who formed ourselves into a committee for the purpose of watching the movements of the British soldiers and gaining every intelligence of the movements of the Tories."

—Paul Revere

Watching the quick and unpredictable movements of cars and people in a congested city is a skill. People are also grouchier in the city. Take, for example, my trip through the Lincoln Highway to get here—mile after mile of nothing. Nope, no people fighting out here in the country. Three days before, on a Friday night, Temple University was on CNN News for having a flash mob. Up to 100 juveniles would suddenly appear and surround a pedestrian, then beat and rob them. When the police did arrive after the third assault, the juveniles turned on the police. It was reported that even one police horse had been punched in the jaw.

When you are in an unfamiliar town, it's important to scope out the area and the people to understand what you are dealing with. The first patriot intelligence network on record was a secret group known as the Mechanics, which meant skilled workers, i.e., Mechanicsburg, a township with skilled workers. The Mechanics were also known as the Liberty Boys. Paul Revere was a part of this group, and is known as the patron of the CIA because of his ability to scope things out.

I'm following his example today. If one takes an analytical view of an adversarial situation, it is possible to distance yourself from emotionally freaking out as the obstacles come flying at you. This teen flash mob was a new heightened sort of mean for Philly, but not unusual. One blogger by the name of Kid Philly said about the area:

> "Temple is in North Philly, actually not too far from Center City, but honestly the neighborhood that surrounds Temple is not great, to say the least. Temple has done a much better job of policing the area and buying up all places it can in the perimeter, but it is an urban setting and close to some of the worst ghettos in the country. Philly overall is like Boston in many ways, with worse neighborhoods and a bigger city. I think mostly Temple is safe, but caution in the urban area is required, as well as where you might choose to live. There are areas close to the campus that have high levels of crime. So, I think it is fair balance to say Temple can be safe with some smart city choices, so to speak. I did just read that the campus received a huge sum of money for expansion, and Center City is slowly gentrifying out that direction."

Since Temple is in the middle of a city, red flags with a large "T" mark where the university begins and ends. There is no majestic gate as your drive through; it is part of the Philadelphia landscape. As I continue to drive, a woman dressed in a long red trench coat wanders aimlessly down at the center solid double yellow line, one foot in front of the other. I missed hitting her. A block later, two young men walked right out in front of traffic on a crosswalk without a green light, thinking that they were Moses or something; that traffic would just part. When we did not slam on our brakes for them, they flipped us off.

Another block up the road, a black cape flapping in the wind caught my eye. A man on a bicycle with his black jacket unzipped was darting in and out of traffic. One minute he was there, the next minute he vanished in between cars. It was very much like a video game, only with much higher stakes.

I think to myself, *Okay, you son-of-a-bitch, where are you going to pop out now?* My hands were gripping the steering wheel so tight that my knuckles were white. Spotting a parking garage instead, I ducked in to safety and from having to make one more split second decision. I paid the seventeen dollars to park, turned off the engine, melted into my seat, and breathed out air I had been holding in for three and a half miles.

LOOKING FOR JESUS

"Our Constitution was made only for a moral and religious people."

—John Adams

Philadelphia has some of the most incredible churches. There were giant cathedrals touching high into the clouds, with massive stained glass windows and crosses that sat atop magnificently-adorned roofs, each beckoning its citizens to come and praise God, truth, good and beauty. Each pronouncing "Euaggelion,"—the good news that the Messiah has risen, offering hope to people of the world.

Catholic Mass used to be said in Latin. Carpe Veratatum means to seize the truth, and that is, after all, what love is—truth. And that is what I spread all day long, every day—truth. I really do feel like an apostle going to town after town, just handing out the Constitution, free market economics policies, *The Law* by Batiste, and gathering up the people that want to join the fellowship. Mother Teresa said, "I am but a small pencil in the hand of a writing God," and so am I. I took a deep breath, grabbed my things, and went out into the chaos. I stand waiting in lines for cross walk signals, let people cut in line, and gave extra coins to beggars. I stopped and listened to a woman who was so lonely she was talking to a light pole. I did whatever I could to let people know they were relevant, because it seemed to me that with all the noise and honking and aggression, that many did not feel relevant.

Today, the club I was with decided to hand out The American Constitution and the Declaration of Independence. We stood out in the cold, wind blowing hard, and handed out about two hundred in about an hour. We could have gone quicker if half the students did not walk around us like we were handing out the plague. It's raining bad today, with cold and icy wind. More winter days appear now, shoving out the warm fall ones. Kevin is on another side of the campus today with another club. He texted me.

Miserable drive over to Temple today, I am with a club working on numbers. We are huddling under a small overhang. Feels like we are hiding in the shadows.

The visual of those two huddled together under the overhang with rain coming down and shivering doubled me over with laughter. The ridiculousness of this situation is just killing me. What else is there to do but laugh? I just kept imagining two wet and dejected puppies out in the rain, and it was an image that was both sweet and sad.

There was not a lot of student interaction for either club today. Maybe it was the cold. With hands jammed in their pockets, shoulders hiked up to their ears, and scarves wrapped and flapping in the wind, they were each so inside themselves and not open. Savannah, who I was with, told me that the students got bothered all the time by people soliciting them for different things, so it was not entirely an aversion to the founding documents—it was just wanting to be left alone, but I still think this is a problem in the world today.

PERSPECTIVE IS
EVERYTHING

"Under all those disadvantages no men ever show more spirit or prudence than ours. In my opinion nothing but virtue has kept our army together through this campaign."

—Colonel John Brooks

By two in the afternoon, we were done with our mission for the day. As I drove home, I passed by the Valley Forge sign I had passed for months, but decided today was the day. I had time to do some "speed tourism." That is, to run, read, and snap photos really fast.

I really did not remember much about Valley Forge from my elementary school history class, but only remembered it for the cool name. "Valley Forge," I said out loud.

It is a beautiful place. There are rolling hills with rich green grass, and Birch, Aspen and Maples line the roadways. I saw where Martha and George stayed, and where the headquarter offices were. Then I began reading a plaque.

"Valley Forge was the military camp 18 miles Norwest of Philadelphia, where the American Continental Armey spent the winter to -1778 during the American Revolutionary war. Starvation, disease, malnutrition and exposure killed more than 2,500 American soldiers by the end of February 1778."

Wha? I thought. *They lost before the battle even began, two-thousand five-hundred soldiers died without firing a shot? No wonder it got attention in the history books, it was a giant failure.*

I had my own failure later when I tried to get out of the Valley Forge area. It was seventeen dollars to park, fifteen dollars to get off the turn pike (wrong turn), then thirty-eight dollars to get back off it at the wrong place again. I was having a huge fight with Little Miss GPS. Because she did not know any different about exorbitant toll fees, she kept telling me to get on where I did not want to. "Recalculating, recalculating, recalculating," she said for over an hour as I tried different approaches.

By the time I got on the right track again, it was dark, and my cognitive decision making abilities were greatly diminished to say the least. I pulled over into a turn pike rest stop. There were a lot of fed-up and worn-out people like me. Huge eighteen-wheelers were lined up like dominoes. Drivers were asleep in the back of their cabs and cars on the other side of the parking lot, tucked in under trees or by fences, windows steamed up with sleep. I'm too tired to drive the two hours' home, so I will sleep here.

I did not sleep too poorly. Each time the windows started to freeze over and I felt the cold hand of the night grab and wake me, I would start the car. This happened about every forty-six minutes, which kept me awake but comfortable. Whenever I got uncomfortable I reminded myself that I could be a soldier at Valley Forge.

WHY SIGN UP FOR A CLUB?

"If we can prevent the government from wasting the labors of the people, under the pretense of taking care of them, they must become happy."

—Thomas Jefferson

They say that humans today have an attention span of 3 seconds. That is less than a goldfish. Combine that with instant gratification and the lost art of conversation, and you have got yourself an uphill battle to get your point across. I treat it like a game, though. If I lose someone, it must be my fault for not having listened to their real concerns.

Today at the university I was confronted with a familiar argument. "What about socialized medicine? What about health care for everyone?" He was a young man of about twenty years old. Inwardly I took a breath and prayed yet again for God to give me the gift of short oratory, which is to make an incredible accurate, compelling, complete and short argument fast. I often fantasize about being blessed with this talent like Einstein, G.K Chesterton, C.S Lewis, Lincoln, and Reagan. And so, find a quick and snappy argument.

"Because you eventually run out of other people's money," I said with a smile on my face. He did not like that, and waited for more, so I dug deeper. It's a risk, but I did it.

"Look, we have already toyed with socialism, most recently in 1927. There was a push for socialism. Norman Thomas was an American Presbyterian minister who achieved fame as a socialist, pacifist, and six-time presidential candidate for the Socialist Party of America. He said that America would never vote for socialism, but under the name of liberalism, people would adopt every aspect of it. The more traditional methods of imposing statism on people had failed, but if it could be done with medicine, it would work. After all, who is going to be against helping the sick? Once the foot was in the door, indefinite expansion could be achieved."

He still was not satisfied and said, "Go on."

So I did. "Now, let's think of the doctor in a socialized medicine system. He loses his freedom, doesn't he? To have patients equally divided geographically, the government would tell a doctor he cannot live where he wants to because they already have enough doctors there. This is a short step to dictating where he will go to work and live. Do any of us have a right to dictate others? I would not like government to dictate to me where I could work. Soon it would be dictating to my children—what trade they will have and where they can live and go to school."

He said, "Well those are things I have not heard of before."

I said, "That's right! That is precisely the reason you join a club—to hear the whole story, all sides. If you're studying to be a doctor, you don't want to just learn half of biology, do you?"

He looked at me and said, "I guess you're right"

I had him. He was thinking. That is all I ask that people do—think. He paused and thought, so I went in for the kill.

"Now, the reason you're in college is to hear both sides. I have just presented you with a side you just admitted you had not heard before. When you join a club, it gives you access to a balanced education. Hearing both sides, you now have equal bits of information and can now make a critical and balanced choice because you now have all the information and not just half of it. That is what students pay for—an education, not an indoctrination.

He said, "Where do I sign up?"

A SMALL TOWN WITH
A BIG HISTORY

"But what is government itself, but the greatest of all reflections on human nature. If men were angels, no government would be necessary. If angels were to govern men, neither external nor internal controls on government would be necessary. In forming a government which is to be administered by men over men, the great difficulty lies in this: you must first enable government to control the governed; and in the next place oblige it to control itself."

—James Madison, The Federalist No. 51

S he had taken his body against the family's will and sold it to the borough (town) back in 1953, and the law suit against the borough only ended recently in 2015. Mauch Chunk was a forgotten, small, quaint mountain railroad borough in need of an attraction. Patricia Thorpe, Jim Thorpe's third wife, sold his body to them, even though he had never been there. Jim Thorpe, a Native American and a native of Oklahoma, was one of the most versatile athletes of modern sports. He won Olympic gold medals in the 1912 pentathlon, decathlon, and played professional football, basketball and baseball. The borough of Mauch Chunk has been known as the borough of Jim Thorpe ever since.

Jim Thorpe is my destination on Sunday, so I can drop down southward and visit four universities on my way down the state. As I enter the borough, I visit the jail. It is a magnificent structure, two stories in height, and known as the place where the hangings of seven Molly Maguire's took place on June 21, 1877. Known locally as the Day of the

Rope, seven Irish coal miners who were Molly Maguires were hanged on the gallows for murder.

Historians believe they were falsely accused, and that the trial of the Molly Maguires was a surrender of state sovereignty, since a private corporation initiated the investigation through a private detective agency, a private police force, and private attorneys, all employees of the company. The Commonwealth of Pennsylvania provided only the courtroom and gallows.

I leave the jail thoroughly disgusted with man's inhumanity towards man. I look up on the top of a hill and see a startlingly familiar mansion. It was the home of Asa Packard, and his mansion was copied by Disney as the haunted mansion. Yep, I am not kidding. That mansion you have all visited in either Disneyland or Disney World is real. It was built by Asa Packard, who was the founder of Lehigh Valley Railroad and Lehigh University. He served as a member of the Pennsylvania House of Representative from 1843–1844. He was a judge of Carbon County, and even ran for president. According to the tour guide, he was the third richest man in America behind Carnegie and Vanderbilt. As the tour guide went on, he said Packard was a Democrat, and did not much like Lincoln or his ideas. Lincoln, as a Republican, opposed slavery, but needed to respect the sovereignty of each state. Lincoln told the Democrats, "You think slavery is right and should be extended, while we think it is wrong and should be limited. That, I suppose, is the trouble. It surely is the only important difference between us." The Democrats feared Lincoln's election. They feared the Republicans winning control of Congress and the Supreme court, and as a result, their right to live their lives as they wished, unfettered by the federal government and the freedom to do whatever they wanted, including owning slaves.

The tour of the Packard Mansion and the tiny borough got me to thinking; man's inhumanity to man seems not to be if you're a Native American, an Irish Molly Maguire or certain political party. It finds a reason. Thank God we live in a country where positive change is possible. With the civil rights movement, America made a move to become what the Declaration of Independence and Constitution had intended.

THE GREAT OUTDOORS

"The cause of America is in a great measure the cause of all mankind."

—Thomas Paine

The velocipede was a wooden contraption with two steel wheels, pedals, and a fixed gear system. It was known as the "bone shaker." The rider was in for a bumpy ride. Today they are known as bicycles, and I love them. I mean, like, *love* 'em. It had been months since I taught a stationary bicycle class at my local gym, and my legs were aching to get on one. The bike train in Jim Thorpe was one of the main reasons I had ventured up so high in the state of Pennsylvania to begin my week's work.

I rented a bike and boarded the train. After attempting to talk to several people and realizing I was just annoying them, I decided to sit down, shut up, and look out the window. I was so excited to go on this trip that I did not pack much—some water, a soft apple, some protein bites, and that's it. No extra phone battery, no extra food, no first aid kit, nothing. Little Miss Ever-Ready and Always Planning had her head up her ass this go around, and ventured out into the wild with not much.

I got my rental bike and took off. There was a whole herd of us all "bunch biking." we were all over the road initially, tripping over one another. As each of us tried to pass the slower riders, the faster ones could be heard yelling "Left" so that the slower ones would move over.

The pamphlet read that it would be a twenty-five-mile bike ride, which I did not think sounded bad, since I biked twice that long regularly. I was free. The woods smelled like wet alder leaves, river, and moss. The air was crisp and clean with a slight smell of smoke from a wood stove off in the distance. The bike trail ran all along the Lehigh river with a smattering of wooden bridges and rock walls. The scenery was gorgeous. I sped up and slowed down as it suited me, then suddenly I realized I was alone. Lost in thought, I looked up and noticed that there were no more bikes in front of me. I slowed down. There were no more bikes behind me. I sped up for miles. No one. I slowed down and even stopped. No one.

Did I not notice a turn? I thought to myself.

I peddled more. Same thing—nothing in front and nothing behind me. No people and no bikes. I was lost. What did I bring to tied me over? Nothing. No food, no first aid kit, and no back-up battery for my dying phone. The sun was setting fast and the storm clouds were pregnant with rain. *How stupid can you get! You're the one who is always supposed to be ready, and you let yourself fall into complacency.*

No sooner had I begun to imagine my feet being amputated from frost bite after walking miles in the snow, emaciated from lack of food and weeks of starvation when I saw my first set of bikes. Note to self: Don't ever leave home so ill prepared ever again, ever. Your safety is your responsibility, Suzanne, and not someone else's.

JUST WHO IS AIRBNB ANYWAY?

"It is very imprudent to deprive America of any of her privileges. If her commerce and friendship are of any importance to you, they are to be had on no other terms than leaving her in the full enjoyment of her rights."

—Benjamin Franklin

In 2007 two guys named Brian and Joe decided to rent out two air beds in their San Francisco apartment, since all hotels were booked and overflowing. That is how Airbnb was born. As I had said earlier, I was not familiar with Airbnb until my three-month assignment in Pennsylvania. We were told to use them, and so I downloaded the app onto my phone.

Tonight, in the town of Jim Thorpe, I met Alexander and his mother, Anna—two Russian immigrants. They are always booked, and I am lucky to have a room tonight. They serve the same thing to every guest—Borscht. It is a classic Russian beet soup, and uses a lot of vegetables with a touch of bacon for extra flavor. It is served to me with a dollop of sour cream and dill weed as a garnish. After dinner I am served a layered chocolate banana cake. They are wonderful hosts. I learn a lot about Russia from Alexander; he tells me how the government is horrible and often pays its employees in liquor, and about the long history of alcoholism that has plagued his country. He says the government has high taxes on alcohol and uses it as revenue, so it does not really want to stop drinking. He says that Putin that is trying to slow the alcoholism rate. "Who knows?" he says. I share with them about life in California and living in the Sierra Nevadas, and what it's like to grow grapes for wine making, and the long hot summers.

Alexander and Anna rely on the income from a full schedule of Airbnb guests, so positive reviews are super important to their livelihood. Often, they sell the houses they live in after they have remodeled them, and move on to another home and do it all again. In older small towns like Jim Thorpe, there are plenty of these sorts of homes. Anna does not speak much English and relies on Alexander. They have found a way to make both an income for themselves and to make the community better, but I am worried for them, and frankly all my hosts.

There is an attack by government on Airbnbs. This past October New York legislation has decided to crack down on Airbnbs. They say that many of their hosts are offering their apartments illegally. To encourage people to comply, Andrew Cuomo, the state governor, approved fines for those who break the rules—$1,000 for the first offense, and then rising to $7,500 for recidivists.

Fredrick Hayek warned in his famous book, *The Road to Serfdom*, the danger of tyranny. It inevitably results from government control of economic decision-making through central planning. The abandonment of individualism inevitably leads to a loss of freedom and the creation of an oppressive society.

Fascism, national socialism, or the popular democratic socialism all have their roots in a centralized economic planning, thereby empowering the state over the individual. I would keep a close eye on this regulation, because as Americans we are grounded in the believe that the government should serve its citizens and not the citizen to serve the government.

AH, TO BE YOUNG AGAIN

"We must take human nature as we find it, perfection falls not to the share of mortals."

—George Washington

Lehigh University is spectacular. There is the library and the church, all dedicated by the Packards to different Packards from the Asa Packard family. It all made sense now that I had visited Jim Thorpe first. There are massive buildings of stone and brick with gargoyles hanging off each spiral, and an enormous cathedral window that seemed as if Quasimodo himself would jump out from a bell tower yelling "Sanctuary, sanctuary!" I tried to push the door open of the church, and it was locked. That's unusual, I thought, for a church. Traditionally, they are left open and ready to receive lost souls. I asked a young fellow sitting on a small rock wall, "Excuse me? Do you know when the church is open?" I asked knowing full well he would not know, because too many young people don't know the origins of buildings and their meanings, and that is a true crime. He said that he didn't know, and so I walked on and finished my day of work.

Late in the day I met with Derek at the top of the stairs of a two-story brown stone. This was one of the cheapest Airbnbs I had stayed at, and for thirty dollars a night I had a mattress on the floor, a blanket and a heater, access to a bathroom, and that was good enough. I felt like a college kid again.

Derek was your typical artist type if ever there was one. He had purple hair, a very nice shirt with a bow tie, red pants that had an inseam that started at the knee, and Converse shoes on. He looked like a clown without the makeup, but I did not say so because fashion is a double-edged sword these days. On the one hand, if you think someone looks like a clown, you say nothing because they are just expressing themselves. But what if they want to look like a clown, and you don't say anything about their costume that they worked so hard on? I am not sure what you do in that situation. In any case, he greeted me with the cutest, thick Australian accent. "Howdy, Suzanne!"

Derek was from Australia, and had been traveling around the U.S. for a few years. He was in the movie-making business somehow. Not sure about that. His girlfriend Marie greeted me as well; I think she was visiting. This is the very first young couple I have stayed with—about thirty years my junior. Looking at them, and how happy and giddy and touchy they were with each, other I began to think of something I had not thought of in months—sex. Up to this moment, I don't think I thought about what a contrast it is to be young. From where I was to where I am now, how you forget about certain things as you age—things that were once so important—get diminished or forgotten about. It's kind of ironic spending so much time around college youth.

I never came into their world till now, not really. As I worked, I listened to them or interviewed them if they wanted to start a club or join one, but I don't think I took the time to go back in time. Where was my brain at? While I was with them I listened more than I talked, but talked enough to share and make them feel comfortable. Marie went to Muhlenberg College and was studying business. She seemed a little more cynical and worldly opposed to Derek's openness and enjoyment of people. I think that is what is so interesting to me about young people this age—they see the brokenness of the world and they want a shot at fixing it. They are so filled with passion, and I think they often mistake that passion for sex when it really is a passion for life in general—a desire to really do something great with their lives. They are impatient and eager for something great to happen.

WHAT IS A SPEECH BALL?

"If freedom of speech is taken away, then dumb and silent we may be led, like sheep to the slaughter."

—George Washington

W hen you say "The Sixties," people generally think the youth movement—peace, love Berkley, and rebellion. That is what a speech ball is; it is a way to rebel against the politically correct police. It is a way to rebel against those who may have had good intentions at one time but have morphed into monsters muzzling anyone that opposes their ideology.

A speech ball is an activism tool; it is an eight-foot-tall beach ball, and hey by the way, who doesn't like beach balls, right? Student club members advocating for free speech and the protection of the First Amendment hand out big black markers and invite other students to write whatever they want, uncensored by others. This means that I cannot cross out what you say, and you cannot cross out what I say. As the student listens, a smile comes over their face. There's a twinkle in their eye. They're like a kid released with a crayon and a clean white wall to write on.

What's fascinating about this project is how unifying it is. While some writes "Fuck Trump" on one side, others write "I am with Her" on the opposite side. Both students look at each other and laugh in unity, realizing the other's humanity. They begin to realize through this exercise that diversity of thought and tolerance for others' opinions mean something. My hope is that they understand that this philosophy was only possible, and I will say that again, ONLY POSSIBLE, in America due to the hindsight of the founders though the creation of First Amendment.

As the hours pass the ball fills with all sorts of thoughts, a math formula, a picture of someone's cat, and "I love fried chicken." But there are the darker writings as well. "Stalin had it right," "Capitalism is evil," and "God Bless Hitler."

The speech ball was developed as a way to fight censorship. Over the past few decades, university campuses have increasingly moved away from teaching to indoctrinating. This has spawned the growth of groups such as the Foundation for Individual Rights in Education, FIRE.

"An overwhelming majority of colleges and universities across the country deny students the rights they are granted under the First Amendment or institutional promises. Every year, FIRE reads through the rules governing student speech at more than 400 of our nation's biggest and most prestigious universities to document the institutions that ignore students' rights—or don't tell the truth about how they've taken them away. FIRE's Spotlight database will tell you if your school is one of them."

Today I am at the University of Pennsylvania in Philadelphia and only feet away from where the majestic statue of Benjamin Franklin sits at the center of University Square. The messages on the ball today are mostly uplifting—only a few have written that Capitalism is Evil or Stalin Had It Right. It is much better than yesterday's speech ball at Temple, I think. I counted at least ten hammer and sickles.

Karl Marx's idea was that "stuff" for everyone would make the world better, and as I read many posts, that is what the youth are focused on. But a new rebellion of youth is needed to rebel against a culture that says to fill up their lives with propaganda and the goods of the world— money, sexual pleasure, power, and fame. Rightfully, the longing of the heart is to be unified with each other and family; only radical love for one another will actually make people fulfilled and happy. I think laughing and writing silly stuff around a big fat ball might crack open the door to this realization.

THE LAST SHOT FIRED

"The American war is over; but this far from being the case with the American revolution. On the contrary, nothing but the first act of the drama is closed. It remains yet to establish and perfect our new forms of government, and to prepare the principles, morals, and manners of our citizens for these forms of government after they are established and brought to perfection."

—Benjamin Rush

It is interesting to note the things we Americans commemorate and the things we do not. For example, on November 19th I was in Gettysburg, and I did not notice one banner or bulletin announcing an honoring of the reading of The Gettysburg Address. Lincoln, on that very day one-hundred and fifty-three years ago, spoke it and reinforced what it means to be an American. However, Haywood County, which is a little county east of the Mississippi, celebrates the last shot fired in the Civil war. They hold a reenactment to mark this event in history. I wonder what history will tell of the events of the election of 2016 and some of the ugliest fighting I have ever seen.

November 7, 2016. Tomorrow is election day. As the world sits and waits in anticipation of who will be the next leader of the free world, there is a numbness. After months and months of battles, families divided and ripped apart due to fierce fighting, the world will know. It has been a long and arduous journey. Debates, phone calls, letters and door knocking as competitors for the position of president of the United States have fallen away over the months. The final hours are upon us.

And it all really is a miracle that we can decide such things by not firing a shot, but through the very civilized act of voting. The only thing the world knew up to 1790 was to murder the monarch or tyrant you despised. Power was not voted on, but was passed down to those at the top within the elite circles. We almost lost it with the Civil War, but regained our balance, and since then we decide our differences by voting. But don't be mistaken. Cheating, lying and winning at all costs has not gone out of style, but the amazing fact remains—that tomorrow someone will win without a shot being fired.

I have decided to take the day off from my conventional job and do the work that others have tirelessly done all along. Known as a battleground state, Pennsylvania, the Keystone State, has participated in all 57 presidential elections through 2012. Barack Obama won over Mitt Romney by about 5%. While still an important prize, with 20 electoral votes, Pennsylvania, like any industrial northern state, has seen the population migrate away in recent decades, resulting in a loss of 45 percent of its electoral clout in 80 years.

As I walk into the Harrisburg election headquarters, I meet Jeff. He is a retired Army Lieutenant Colonel, and in charge. He barks orders out with such glee that he reminds me of what Patton would look like ordering small school children around. Most of the volunteers are older. This does not surprise me. As Churchill has been attributed to stating, "If you are not a liberal when you are 25, you have no heart. If you are not a conservative by the time you are 35, you have no brain."

What this does demonstrate to me is that politics truly does go to those that show up, and if we don't get the candidate we want we have no one to blame but ourselves for our lack of involvement. I will do what I can, and I regret not doing more, as the battle has been fierce this past year. Our office picks up those who cannot get to the polling booths— the Amish, the disabled; we stuff envelopes and make calls. I will stay until the final hours, and until the last door is knocked on, and the last shot fired.

SOME MOVIES ARE WORTH WATCHING

"*It is not necessary to enumerate the many advantages that arise from this custom of early marriages. They comprehend all the society can receive from this source; from the preservation, and increase of the human race. Everything useful and beneficial to man, seems to be connected with obedience to the laws of his nature, the inclinations, the duties, and the happiness of individuals, resolve themselves into customs and habits, favourable, in the highest degree, to society. In no case is this more apparent, than in the customs of nations respecting marriage.*"

—Samuel Williams

I t is rare for me to watch a movie, since in my view someone else thought of it, wrote it and created it. They did something while I am relegated to being a non-participating receiver. But good stories we love teach us life lessons. This evening, exhausted from work and needing an escape, I scrolled through the list of old movies from Amazon on my laptop and found this review for a movie called *Still Mine*, which piqued my interest.

"I'm a man in my seventh decade of life who has seen much and who has experienced much. This movie, I found quite by accident, but I'm much richer from having found it! I had not seen the actress in any role in years; I do not know why; perhaps I just had not found her movies, nor the male lead in several years; but, again, I am enormously glad to have found them partnered in these roles. I caught many lumps in my throat in several scenes, and the acting was so natural as to be a real event, which I was sharing all the way through. I cannot thank you enough for allowing access to this movie. While it broke my heart, it also was quite healing; and I could only hope that someone (anyone) might love me so much as that affection and deep-soul type love that was so manifest in this movie. I would honestly give it 10 stars, if that many were available to me. As my title suggests: It was not one's ideal of a "thrilling" movie, but it was certainly one that will touch your heart—and even your soul, if you have one that can be touched. I would gladly watch it again; and that is how I judge an excellent movie."

I rented the movie, watched it, and found that it was the best kind—a true story. True stories don't have an agenda; they just are. This is the story of an elderly man's effort to build his wife a new home. Now suffering from dementia, the older home has become outdated and too much to handle. As a master craftsman, the house he builds is magnificent, but built without permits. An overzealous and dispassionate bureaucrat enjoying his authority a bit too much and seeing only the letter of the law and not the spirit of the law creates a living hell and a miserable life for the protagonist. Meanwhile, the middle-aged and over-concerned daughter does her best to further create anguish for her father by urging him to get a builder and get it done in two weeks.

The father snaps back at her, "I don't want a builder, I am enjoying creating this. It is giving me my sense of purpose and dignity to build this for your mother, I need to do this."

I won't ruin the movie for you, but suffice to say it has some big lessons in it about big government. I thoroughly enjoyed it.

THE NIGHT
THE WORLD EXPLODED!

"The most effectual engines for (pacifying a nation) are the public papers. (A despotic) government always (keeps) a kind of standing army of news writers who, without any regard to truth or to what should be like truth, (invent) and put into the papers whatever might serve the ministers. This suffices with the mass of the people who have no means of distinguishing the false form the true paragraphs of a newspaper."

—Thomas Jefferson to G.K. van Hogendorp, Oct. 13, 1785

It was 2 a.m. I could not sleep, probably because I was in my car again, I had gotten used to it, kind of. I had become accustom to the low rates of the Airbnbs, and so hotel prices felt like a small down payment on a mortgage. I just could not do it. The way they said "One-hundred and twenty dollars, please," as easily as they said twenty-five cents made me want to smack 'em right up side of the head.

"What?" I muttered, "To be unconscious?" If I spent that much money, I would like to remember it at least! So, it was easier to just pull off the road and close my eyes for a bit of long rest at the Marriot hotel parking lot. I knew I was safe there.

Kevin had agreed to take me to Independence Hall no matter the outcome of the election. It was one of the last things on my list of things to see in Pennsylvania. I was finally going to see it, and how fitting to see it the day after election. Kevin and I agreed to meet somewhere close enough to old town Philadelphia. The plan was to drop off my car and take his so he could drive through the maze of traffic, which he knew so well being a native Pennsylvanian.

This would be my last time in Philadelphia, I reasoned. With only a few days left to go, I had accomplished my mission. Getting a commitment from him to take me so late in the day would mean that I would have to spend the night again in the area. It was too far to go home and too late to find an Airbnb, so I would be spending one last night—election night—in my car.

I reclined my chair, threw the blanket over my head, grabbed my cell phone, and made a little tent like you do when you're a kid, only without the comic books and marshmallow crème. This night was election night. I hit refresh on my cell phone every half hour to see who was winning the battle. It looked like she was winning for hours, and then something astonishing happened at midnight. The numbers skewed and had him skyrocket up on the little graph I was looking at. The distance between the two would only increase as the minutes and hours went by, and by 2 a.m. it was clear who had won war.

I thought to myself, *He did it. No freaking way. He beat them all. He beat the party machine, the entire mass media, including the network that was supposed to be on his side, he beat the Never Trump movement, he beat established political veterans and the overwhelming favorite, Bush. He beat voter fraud and sexual assault allegations, he beat Access Hollywood, and he beat a formidable candidate. The only greater victory was in 1776.*

And Pennsylvania had just put Donald Trump over the top!!!

I watched until my eyes grew heavy and the phone dropped from my hands onto my chest. I did not wake again until the morning and the sun shone in through my windshield. Last night was a real November surprise for a lot of people. In the biggest political upset of our lifetime, the American people elected Donald J Trump and Mike Pence to lead our nation. I turned on my phone once again, wiped the sleep from my eyes, and watched as the media struggled to regain its credibility, sounding smart and dignified while reporting on the explosion that just happened all over them. Failure and lost credibility dripped from their faces, business suits and cocktail dresses. The biggest thing to come from the battle was that the media—all of them including radio, television and print—just demonstrated just how self-serving they are and just how disconnected they are from the citizens they are purported to represent.

Victory speeches began pouring in from across the country. Lincoln's party, the Republican party, won big across the nation, winning the House, Congress and Governorships. Mia Love who won in Utah sent out a statement:

> "What a great day for Utah and our country. Thank you so very much for the love and support you have given our family. I am certain that decades from now, a history book will contain a chapter on the events of today 2016 and the destinational decisions that were placed before the American people. When our grandchildren point to those pages in the history books, each of us today will be able to proudly and confidently say, 'I was there! We looked fear in the face and then stood up with courage and did our part to create a better Utah and a better America.' Thank you. God bless you all and God bless our still-independent United States of America."

A statement from Minister Franklin Graham who had gone on a state-to-state prayer crusade at each capital:

> "This election has been long, it's been tough, and it's been divisive. It's time to put that behind us. Now is the time to come together in unity and work together. Our nation has so many problems that need fixing. Even more important are the spiritual needs of our country. Whether we are rich or poor, without Jesus Christ we are the most desperately in need, the poorest of the poor. We cannot ignore His hand and His supreme authority.
>
> One thing is for sure, we need to pray for our new president, vice president, and our other leaders every day—whether we agree with them or not. They need God's help and direction. It is my prayer that we will truly be one nation under God. Will you commit with me to pray for them every day?"

It was over. After nearly two long years, it was finally over. I suppose that in the end, we wrangle about the same stuff as the founders did since the forming of the Constitution—states' rights versus federal rights and the limits of executive authority. It is every generation's responsibility to know the details of these issues and then act—and to vote.

A VISIT TO OLD LIBERTY

"From such an Assembly can a perfect production be expected? It therefore astonishes me, Sir, to find this system approaching so near to perfection as it does; and I think it will astonish our enemies, who are waiting with confidence to hear that our councils are confounded like those of the Builders of Babel; and that our States are on the point of separation, only to meet hereafter for the purpose of cutting one another's throats. Thus I consent, Sir, to this Constitution because I expect no better, and because I am not sure, that it is not the best."

—Benjamin Franklin

The next morning, as I opened the car door and my feet hit the ground, I heard things crack and squeak in my body I had never heard before. I went inside the turnpike service plaza to take my usual sink shower and brush my teeth. I ordered breakfast, flipped open my laptop, and began work.

I looked down at my phone. Nope, no word from Kevin. That's okay. It's only 6:00 a.m. An hour later, no word. Another hour, no word. It gets to eight in the morning and I text him, *hey Kevin, where are we meeting?*

Kevin: *Oh hey, you still want to go?*

What the hell? Why would I not want to go? I just spent the night in my freaking car again just so that I could go! Lord give me strength. Young people! I text him back, *yes, I still want to go!*

We were on our way. I was finally going to see Independence Hall, known as America's most historic square mile, and it seemed fitting to go see this historic place where it all began the day after one of the most historic elections in our history. We got our tickets and stood in line. Suddenly, a loud and commanding voice told us to spit out our gum, throw away our water or food, and listen-up! Instinctively, we all snapped to attention, even though I am sure many had never been in the military. The ranger began, "The guides have put a lot of work into their presentations, so please be quiet and have some respect." I looked around, but saw no one, but then my eye caught a little hat move at the edge of the crowd. It was a dwarf ranger, and he looked like he would kick all our asses if we did not do what he said, so we did. We all spit out our gum, shut up, and sat down. The tour guide began.

Independence Hall is where both the United States Declaration of Independence and the United States Constitution were debated and adopted. It is now the centerpiece of the Independence National Historical Park in Philadelphia and a World Heritage Site. Built in 1753 as the colonial legislature, it became the meeting place for the Second Continental Congress from 1775 to 1783 and was the site of the Constitutional Convention in the summer of 1787.

As we walked through the rooms, it was easy to visualize George Washington or Ben Franklin walking on these wooden floors, grabbing a chair and sitting at a table. A fire would roar in the two fireplaces as ideas were discussed. There in the center of the room was Washington's chair, The Rising Sun Armchair, where Washington sat for three months of the Federal Conventions continuous sessions.

After Independence Hall, we headed over to the state house yard where the bells of the city, the Liberty bell, summoned the people to hear the reading of the Declaration of Independence. Read by Colonel John Nixon, they would at that moment go from being subjects to citizens. Thereby changing world history, they would go from being people who served government to a people who expected government to serve them.

In Congress, July 4th 1776, The unanimous Declaration of the thirteen colonies of the United States of America.

"When in the course of human events it becomes necessary for one people to dissolve the political bands which have connected them with another and to assume among the powers of the earth, the separate and equal station to which the Laws of Nature and of Nature God entitle them...."

On the bell is the biblical inscription from the book of Leviticus 25:10 and it reads, "Proclaim liberty throughout all the land unto all inhabitants thereof."

As we closed out our afternoon, my mind went to how valuable these places are. Actually they are the most valuable of all places in America because they tell a story of who we are at our core; that despite our differences, like a compass that always points north, this sacred ground will always remind Americans that they were the first in the history of the world to govern themselves. This is the great American experiment, and where it happened and why it needs to be visited and contemplated by each American. Heritage is the most valuable thing a person has, and a nation must protect it because it gives us direction when we get lost. The Bible reminds us of this in Proverbs 29:13. "Where there is no vision, the people perish."

My mind can't help but wander back through history at times when people were stripped of their heritage in order to crush them. In 1939 German armies flooded into Poland and began a systematic stripping of their heritage in order to demoralize and confuse. It was an overall effort to destroy Polish culture. Thousands of churches and monasteries were confiscated, closed, or destroyed. Priceless works of religious art and sacred objects were lost forever, and an estimated three thousand priests and intellectuals—anyone capable of passing on heritage—were executed. And today the deliberate theft and destruction of cultural heritage goes on by the Islamic State. In 2014 ISIL blew up The Temple of Baalshamin in Palmyra, which brought worldwide attention to the heinous crime of stripping a people of its culture.

Kevin hits my shoulder and knocks me out of my deep thoughts. "Hey, we need to get you a real Philly cheese steak." I am grateful for the jar back into the present moment. As we walk on cobble stone streets past Christ Church and the Benjamin Franklin Museum, I am filled with a gratitude such as I have never experienced in my life—for this visit, for this friendship, for my nation, and for the genuine Philly cheese steak I am about to eat.

A NOTE FROM COMPATRIOT SAM

I was picked up by a Muslim Uber driver today. I introduced myself. He said his name was Muhammad. I shook his hand. We talked about how beautifully the leaves were turning and about the cold weather awaiting us.

I then shifted the conversation to something colder than the current Virginia breeze. I turned and asked for his opinion on the current political state.

I let him talk and give his opinion. The man was frightened, and a little combative towards my opinion, but we continued. He said that Americans have treated him with more respect than his own people. That here in America, he is free to worship without fear of other Muslim sects. He wept.

As he was dropping me off, I reached over and gave him a hug. He wept still. I told him I was Republican and that I respected his religion, his life, and his rights. I told him not to fear, and have faith. I promised him that nothing would happen to him.

It's always been up to us Americans as individuals to respect and love one another, not government. I did my best to understand him and his fears. People may say that love trumps hate. If this is true, then do it. Go out and love your neighbor. Hug and cry with the one who is frozen with fear. Put aside civics and government and calm their passionate and restless hearts.

Clubs to join or start on your campus:

1. Young Americans for Freedom
2. Turning Point USA
3. Act for America
4. Students for Conceal Carry
5. Love & Fidelity Network
6. Young Women for America
7. Christians United for Israel
8. Students Supporting Israel
9. Young Americans for Liberty
10. Students for Liberty
11. The Federalist Society
12. Students for Life of America
13. The Benjamin Rush Institute
14. Intercollegiate Studies Institute, Educating For Liberty
15. Collegians for a Constructive Tomorrow
16. Network of Enlightened Women
17. STRIVE

Made in the USA
San Bernardino, CA
26 January 2017